Stealing the Initiative

Real Politics in America

Series Editor: Paul S. Herrnson, *University of Maryland*

The books in this series bridge the gap between academic scholarship and the popular demand for knowledge about politics. They illustrate empirically supported generalizations from original research and the academic literature using examples taken from the legislative process, executive branch decision making, court rulings, lobbying efforts, election campaigns, political movements, and other areas of American politics. The goal of the series is to convey the best contemporary political science research has to offer in ways that will engage individuals who want to know about real politics in America.

Stealing the Initiative
How State Government Responds to Direct Democracy

Elisabeth R. Gerber
*University of California, San Diego
and Adjunct Fellow, Public Policy
Institute of California*

Arthur Lupia
University of California, San Diego

Mathew D. McCubbins
University of California, San Diego

D. Roderick Kiewiet
California Institute of Technology

Prentice
Hall

Upper Saddle River, New Jersey 07458

Library of Congress Cataloging-in-Publication Data
Stealing the initiative : how state government responds to direct democracy / Elisabeth R. Gerber … [et al.].
   p. cm.
   Includes bibliographical references.
   ISBN 0-13-028407-6
   1. Referendum—California. 2. California—Politics and government—1951- I. Gerber, Elisabeth R., 1964-
JF495.C2S73 2001
328.2′2′09794—dc21

00-032676
CIP

VP, Editorial Director: Laura Pearson
Director of Marketing: Beth Gillett Mejia
Assistant Editor: Brian Prybella
Editorial Assistant: Beth Murtha
Managing Editor: Ann Marie McCarthy
Production Liaison: Fran Russello
Project Manager: Patty Donovan, Pine Tree Composition
Prepress and Manufacturing Buyer: Ben Smith
Cover Art Director: Jayne Conte
Cover Designer: Kiwi Design
Cover Art: Kiwi Design

This book was set in 10/12 Palatino by Pine Tree Composition, Inc., and was printed and bound by Courier Companies, Inc. The cover was printed by Phoenix Color Corp.

Real Politics in America Series
Paul S. Herrnson, Series Editor

 © 2001 by Prentice-Hall, Inc.
A Division of Pearson Education
Upper Saddle River, New Jersey 07458

Printed in the United States of America
10 9 8 7 6 5 4 3 2 1

ISBN: 0-13-028407-6

Prentice-Hall International (UK) Limited, *London*
Prentice-Hall of Australia Pty. Limited, *Sydney*
Prentice-Hall Canada Inc., *Toronto*
Prentice-Hall Hispanoamericana, S.A., *Mexico*
Prentice-Hall of India Private Limited, *New Delhi*
Prentice-Hall of Japan, Inc., *Tokyo*
Pearson Education Asia Pte. Ltd., *Singapore*
Editora Prentice-Hall do Brasil, Ltda., *Rio de Janeiro*

Contents

Preface

Early in the twentieth century, a few American states began to offer their citizens a larger role in government. Through a process called the *direct initiative*, citizens could write and pass laws without interference from the legislature. As the century progressed, a growing number of states allowed direct initiatives. And as the century closed, more citizens used this opportunity to change state laws. In California alone, voters designed initiatives to slash their taxes, impose term limits, dismantle bilingual education, and replace affirmative action.

Direct initiatives, a form of direct democracy, are controversial. One important controversy concerns the extent to which initiatives influence what government does. Many people believe that initiatives that win on Election Day take effect immediately and affect public policy substantially. There are, however, great variations in what happens to initiatives after they pass. While some take full effect, others do not affect policy at all. What accounts for winning initiatives' widely varying effects?

In *Stealing the Initiative*, our answer to this question builds from an often overlooked fact about the initiative process: government actors must choose to comply with an initiative if it is to affect policy. Every winning initiative gives government actors opportunities to make implementation and enforcement decisions. When making these decisions, they regularly reinterpret, and sometimes reverse, electoral outcomes. Understanding this fact is essential for anyone who wants to explain how voter initiatives affect public policy.

In *Stealing the Initiative*, we examine the conditions under which government does (and does not) comply with winning initiatives. We find that full compliance with initiatives is the exception, rather than the rule. Using examples from real politics, we show that the conditions that must exist for full compliance with an initiative are very difficult to satisfy. If, for example, a legislative majority and the governor are united in their opposition to an initiative, then full compliance with the initiative is extraordinarily un-likely—even if voter support for the initiative was high.

Indeed, we prove that under normal conditions, government actors' policy preferences displace initiative content—at least in part—as the ulti-mate determinant of a winning initiative's policy impact. Our ten case stud-ies reinforce this finding by showing multiple instances where elected representatives who were against popular initiatives in California pre-vented their full implementation. Such actors literally "steal" the initiatives.

Our findings have important implications for the politics of the many states and localities that permit direct initiatives. Consider, for example, the idea that voter initiatives cause legislative gridlock. Our work suggests that the choices of elected officials, rather than the actions of voters, are the more likely cause of such impasses.

Our work also reveals how the actions of future initiative propo-nents—the language they employ, the coalitions they build, and the re-sources they mobilize—will affect their ability to influence public policy. We highlight potential conflicts between the types of initiatives that can pre-vail on Election Day and the types of initiatives that government actors are likely to implement if voters approve them. As a result, we clarify the link between the language that initiative writers choose and their ability to change what government does.

If recent trends are any indication, increasing numbers of people will use direct initiatives in the twenty-first century. This means that initiatives could affect your life in a growing number of ways. It is therefore increas-ingly important to understand how winning initiatives affect public policy. *Stealing the Initiative* sheds new light on this topic.

ACKNOWLEDGMENTS

The authors acknowledge the generous support of this project by the Public Policy Institute of California. We thank Christopher DenHartog for his dedi-cated service to this project, from its inception to its completion. We thank James E. Alt, R. Michael Alvarez, Bruce E. Cain, Jack Citrin, Jack Coons, John Ellwood, Beth Gillett, David Grether, Zoltan Hajnal, Paul Herrnson, Thaddeus Kousser, David Magleby, Kathleen Much, the Public Policy Insti-tute of California research staff, and participants at seminars on this study given at Harvard University, UCLA, and the annual meeting of the Ameri-can Political Science Association (Atlanta, 1999) for valuable suggestions. We also thank Donna Hirsch of the Bureau of the Census for her assistance in obtaining data, Michelle Reinschmidt for preparing figures and tables, and Michael Epstein for research assistance. Professor Kiewiet acknowl-edges the support of the John Randolph Haynes and Dora Haynes Founda-tion. Professors Gerber and Lupia acknowledge the support of the Center for Advanced Study in the Behavioral Sciences, where they completed this study.

1

Introduction

Many citizens describe their state government as unresponsive, acrimonious, or inadequate (Noll 1995, California Citizens Budget Commission 1995). A recent poll in California, for example, finds that for every person in the state who expresses "a lot" of confidence in the state's government, three others had "not much" confidence (Field Institute 1997). Even in a time of historic economic expansion and budget surpluses, many citizens continue to disapprove of their state legislature (see, for example, Field Institute 1999).

Polls are not the only way for citizens to voice their displeasure with government. If they were, then the world would not find the politics of states such as California as intriguing as they are today. But the presence of direct democracy as an outlet for voter frustration provides a most intriguing spectacle.

Since the early 1900s, a growing number of states have allowed citizens to draft and pass their own laws using *direct initiatives*. Direct initiatives are a common form of direct democracy. The distinguishing characteristic of *direct democracy* is that regular citizens, and not elected representatives, make laws by voting on ballot propositions.[1]

As we embark upon a new century, more citizens are taking advantage of the initiative process. In recent years, for example, citizens have used

1

direct initiatives to pass laws on issues such as tax reform, affirmative action, and term limits. Today, 24 states, the District of Columbia, and hundreds of local governments allow direct initiatives.

Polls and initiatives are similar in that they provide venues for voter frustration. They are, however, commonly presumed to have different effects on public policy. When voters voice their frustrations in polls, the effects on policy are indirect at best. Polls cause policy change only if the numbers in the poll cause government actors to change their minds about the merits of existing laws. Most polls have no such effect.

When voters voice their frustration through the initiative process, by contrast, the effects are supposed to be direct. Unlike polls, initiatives are supposed to be "binding" in that laws passed by voters have the same legal standing as laws passed by legislatures. *But how different is the effect of initiatives?*

A common belief about the initiative process is that the path from electoral victory to policy change is simple—if an initiative prevails on Election Day and survives legal challenges regarding its constitutionality, then it prevails as a policy directive.[2] Because this belief is so prevalent, elected representatives and political pundits blame the initiative process for a long list of problems. In years of legislative stalemate, for example, critics blame voter initiatives for tying legislators' hands and delaying legislative negotiations. In years of budget problems, critics blame initiatives for their legislatures' inability to fund certain programs.

Unlike many political criticisms, this one is nonpartisan. Critics from the left, right, and center join political insiders and political outsiders in blaming the initiative process for outcomes they dislike. The initiative process is an easy scapegoat for critics of state politics.

But are these criticisms valid? To what extent do winning initiatives really affect public policy? In what follows, we review evidence supporting the idea that winning initiatives have substantial policy impacts. Then we present a very different view.

REASONS TO BELIEVE THAT WINNING INITIATIVES AFFECT POLICY

Two factors support the notion that winning initiatives influence policy directly and substantially: the large number of initiatives and the style of modern initiative campaigns.

As of 1998, six states had held elections on more than 100 direct initiatives each. Oregon led the way with 300, followed by California (264), Colorado (195), North Dakota (167), Arizona (144), and Washington (124). Oregon also led the way in initiatives passed, with 110. California adopted 90 (34 percent).[3] Oregon's lead in both categories is indicative of a long period of intense initiative activity. Perhaps Oregon should be the state that comes to mind when Americans think about the initiative process, but this is not usually the case.

In recent years, California has surpassed Oregon in the rate at which it uses direct initiatives. In the period from 1979 to 1998, Californians voted on 107 initiatives, of which 47 (44 percent) passed. The states with the next most frequent usage during this period were Oregon (95) and Colorado (70).[4] Rightly or wrongly, California is today the state that most Americans associate with the initiative process.

The relatively large number of initiatives in places like California gives the impression that the process greatly affects public policy. Reinforcing this perception is the style of modern initiative campaigns. Today's campaigns are battles of soundbytes, endorsements, and direct mail—all of which send the same message: Initiatives bring big change.

For example, the managers of "Yes on Proposition X" campaigns tend to choose simple, attention-grabbing themes in their attempts to convince voters that if Proposition X wins on Election Day, a new and substantially better policy will result. At the same time, managers of "No on Proposition X" campaigns work to convince voters that passing the initiative will cause a substantial, and bad, policy change. Neither side in an initiative campaign has an incentive to claim that Proposition X will have little or no effect if it wins.[5]

Initiative campaigners also have an incentive to attract attention to the arguments they make. In many states, proponents and opponents spend large sums of money to publicize their messages. The average cost of an initiative campaign in California in 1998, for example, was $8,401,934 (California Secretary of State 1999). The most expensive cost $66,922,504, and even the least expensive campaign cost more than $400,000. So, unlike political debates in the state legislature, debates over initiatives take place in the public eye—in the newspapers, on television, literally in the public's living rooms and mailboxes. Citizens are therefore likely to be much more aware of initiatives than of regular legislation. Given the content and frequency of initiative campaign messages, voters are also likely to get the impression that an initiative's electoral victory implies a substantial policy change.

A number of studies supply further support for the idea that initiatives have a large effect on policy. For example, California's Proposition 98, passed by voters in 1988, requires that at least 40 percent of the state's general fund be spent on K–14 education. Many observers believe that Proposition 98 has proven to be a binding constraint. It has, for example, forced the hand of the governor and the state legislature at critical moments in budget negotiations—inducing them to protect educational expenditures in cases where they might not otherwise have done so (see, for example, Cain and Noll 1995, Ellwood and Sprague 1995, Kiewiet 1995). A study by the state's Legislative Analyst's Office (LAO) gives a similar impression. In 1990, it estimated that only eight to ten percent of the state's budget was subject to legislative discretion. The rest of the budget was externally directed by a combination of initiatives, federal mandates, and previous legislation (LAO 1990, California Citizens Budget Commission 1995).

In short, the sheer number of initiatives, the style of initiative campaigns, and examples of their effectiveness all combine to give the impression that if winning initiatives survive court challenges, then they force substantial policy change. But does this evidence really indicate the extent to which winning initiatives affect policy? We argue that it does not. To be certain, some initiatives have had a large impact on state policy. Many winning initiatives, however, are never implemented or enforced. We now turn our attention to why this happens.

REASONS FOR DOUBT

From the time the first signatures are collected to the time the final votes are counted, initiative campaign organizations try to convince voters that initiatives will change policy substantially. The post-electoral history of initiatives, however, paints a different picture. Many initiatives that win at the ballot box are challenged in the courts. Between 1960 and 1999, 36 of the 55 initiatives passed by California voters (65 percent) were challenged in state or federal court. Of these, 14 were upheld, 11 were invalidated in part, 7 were invalidated entirely, and 4 remain pending as of this writing (Miller 1999). Court rulings that strike down initiatives tend to be very public and are perceived as the primary obstacle preventing the implementation of winning initiatives.

Less recognized, but just as critical to the fate of winning initiatives, are the often invisible obstacles erected by government actors. Indeed, there is great variation in what government actors do with winning initiatives after they leave the voters' hands. A few take full effect, but many others are never enforced. This happens because *every winning initiative gives government actors an opportunity to make implementation and enforcement decisions.* When making these decisions, government actors regularly reinterpret, and sometimes reverse, electoral outcomes. Understanding this fact is essential for anyone who wants to explain how initiatives affect public policy.

For example, if complying with an initiative entails raising new funds, spending new funds, or reallocating existing funds—as many initiatives do—then the legislature, and not the initiative's authors, must make these funds available (i.e., the legislature must revise previous budget agreements to incorporate a winning initiative's budgetary requirements). In many cases, if the legislature refuses to allocate funds, then no resources are available for implementation, and the initiative dies. Alternatively, if state bureaucrats need instructions about how to implement a winning initiative, some government actor must write the instructions, and the legislature or a high-level bureaucrat must approve them. When the actors responsible for writing instructions choose to ignore the initiative's policy instructions, their actions can have the effect of nullifying the election result.

Thus, we argue that the most important thing to recognize about the post-election fate of voter-approved initiatives is this: *Winning initiatives neither implement nor enforce themselves.* If an initiative is to affect policy, government actors must take an active role in converting winning initiatives into policy changes. If they fail to comply, initiatives die.

WHEN, THEN, DO WINNING INITIATIVES AFFECT POLICY?

To answer this question, it is not sufficient to count the number of winning initiatives or to rely on the oversimplified claims made by initiative proponents and opponents during campaigns. Nor can we rely on the many complaints about initiatives made by political actors who need a scapegoat for the painful trade-offs that modern governance requires. Instead, we need to be able to explain why government actors choose to comply with some initiatives but not with others.

In *Stealing the Initiative*, we examine the implementation and enforcement decisions of government actors, including the governor and the legislature. We use the term *compliance* to refer generically to actors' decisions to implement or enforce initiatives. We consider compliance to be full when government actors implement and enforce an initiative in the way that its authors intended. We consider compliance to be partial when some part of the initiative is reinterpreted or ignored by government actors. We consider there to be no compliance when government actors ignore the initiative entirely. Note that when an actor chooses partial compliance, the reinterpretation need not be detrimental to the initiative proponents' interests. The point is simply that the decisions of government actors change how the words of initiative proponents affect public policy.

Our research on the politics of initiative compliance has two components. First, we examine how government actors' policy desires interact with the political circumstances they face to affect their implementation and enforcement decisions. This examination highlights the basic underlying structural factors of real politics that produce predictable patterns of government behavior from the many and varied situations that winning initiatives encounter.

Then we turn to a series of case studies regarding the post-electoral fates of winning initiatives in California. For each case, we analyze spending and performance data to estimate the extent to which government complied with the initiative in question. The compliance behavior we observe varies dramatically. Most of the initiatives we examine are implemented only partially. Some are not implemented at all.

Indeed, our main finding is that the conditions that must exist for full compliance with an initiative are very difficult to satisfy. If, for example, a legislative majority and the governor are united in their opposition to an initiative, then full compliance is extraordinarily unlikely—even if voter support for the initiative was high. More likely, these government actors will attempt to implement or enforce the initiative only partially, reinterpreting it in ways that are more consistent with their own policy desires and less consistent with the desires of the initiative's proponents.

Our case studies reinforce this conclusion. In particular, they reveal how features of the initiatives themselves—such as the detail with which they are written, the ease of observing compliance, and the stringency of punishments for noncompliance—affect their ultimate policy impact. By so doing, our work reinforces, refines, and extends the important work of scholars such as Pressman and Wildavsky (1984), who examined in great detail the problems inherent in Oakland, California's effort to implement a federal economic stimulus program, and of Bowen and Lee (1979), who documented California's failure to implement a number of pre-Proposition 13 initiatives.

When reading *Stealing the Initiative*, it is important to note that the purpose of our research is neither to condemn policymakers when they choose not to comply fully with winning initiatives, nor to condemn the initiative process when it produces laws that actually bind government actors. Given the broad range of political perspectives among any state's citizens, politicians, policymakers, and political observers, it is not possible to give a broadly satisfying answer as to whether a particular degree of initiative compliance is "good" or "bad." Even we, the authors of this study, are of mixed opinions on the matter. But regardless of whether you love the initiative process or despise it, it is important to be informed about the extent to which winning initiatives affect public policy. And even if you do not live in a state that currently allows initiatives, it is useful to understand that what happens to laws after they pass—whether these laws are written by citizens or state legislatures—is far from automatic. *Stealing the Initiative* sheds new light on both topics.

PLAN OF THE BOOK

Stealing the Initiative continues as follows. In Chapter 2, we briefly describe the initiative process in California—the setting for much of our analysis. Here, we also describe the types of people and groups who are likely to support a winning initiative, as well as why these winners are likely to have conflicting interests with the government officials who will be charged with the initiative's implementation and enforcement. In Chapter 3, we examine the politics of initiative compliance. We use this examination to generate concrete predictions about the extent of initiative compliance in real political cases. In Chapter 4, we turn our attention to case studies and describe how we chose particular cases to study. Chapters 5 through 15 contain the case studies themselves. In each of these chapters, we describe the features of the political environment that affected the post-election fate of the initiative in question. In Chapter 15, our final case study, we provide a detailed analysis of how compliance with California's Proposition 13 of 1978 affected public school funding in the decades that followed. Proposition 13, America's most famous initiative, capped property tax rates and is widely blamed for the decline of school spending in California. Our work calls this account into question. In Chapter 16, we conclude with a statement about what our research implies about the future consequences of direct initiatives. In the end, *Stealing the Initiative* provides an important, but currently unconventional, understanding of how initiatives affect public policy.

NOTES

1. Referendums are the other most common form of direct democracy. The difference between direct initiatives and referendums is this: Initiatives are laws that are *written by citizens* and placed on the ballot by citizen petition. Referendums, by contrast, are laws that are *written by legislatures* and placed on the ballot automatically (i.e., submitted referendums) or by citizen petition (i.e., popular referendums).
2. Initiatives may be either statutory, in that they describe new or amended laws, or constitutional, in that they describe new or amended provisions of constitutions. While the legality of statutory initiatives can be challenged on state constitutional grounds, constitutional initiatives cannot—they become part of the state constitution. See Magleby 1984 for further details.
3. *Source:* Initiative and Referendum Institute, *www.iandrinstitute.org.*
4. *Source:* Initiative and Referendum Institute, *www.iandrinstitute.org.*
5. For initiative proponents, such claims would only call into question why Proposition X is needed. For initiative opponents, such claims would imply that there is little to lose in voting for Proposition X. In both cases, such claims would likely reduce motivation to turn out among voters whose support they desire.

2

Background
on California's
Initiative Process

How does someone's policy idea become a winning initiative? We answer this question by describing the procedures that groups must follow to place their policy proposal before the voters. We discuss current procedures in California, the state in which our case studies are based. Most places that allow the direct initiative follow similar procedures (see DuBois and Feeney 1992 for an interstate comparison).

We follow our description of procedures with a discussion of who succeeds in placing their proposals on the ballot. We also explain why these same people are likely to encounter problems after the election. In short, people and groups who are willing and able to put an initiative on the ballot are also likely to have different policy preferences than the government actors who will be charged with implementing and enforcing their initiative if it wins.

PROCEDURES

The procedures that constitute California's initiative process today reflect the political conditions that were present at its birth. California added provisions for direct initiatives to its Constitution in 1911. Members of the state's Progressive movement were the strongest supporters of this move. Historical accounts indicate that the Progressives wanted to counter the Southern Pacific Railroad's influence over state legislators. They charged that this influence was preventing the state from passing needed economic, political, and social reform legislation.[1] Indeed, accounts from the time report that the wealthy railroad protected its interests by "buying" legislative representation (Mowry 1976). Frustrated by years of stalemate on their own policy agenda, the Progressives championed direct legislation as a way to circumvent an uncooperative state legislature.

While California has changed considerably since 1911, the procedures that citizens must follow to use direct initiatives are much the same today as they were back then. These procedures define three distinct stages in the initiative process: the *drafting* stage, the *qualification* stage, and the *campaign* stage.

The first stage is the *drafting* stage. In theory, any citizen can draft an initiative. In practice, drafting an initiative requires a great deal of expertise or resources sufficient to hire professional consultants. If potential initiative sponsors want their initiative to pass on Election Day, for example, they must know enough about state politics to draft legislation that will attract the support of a broad coalition of voters. If these potential sponsors also want their legislation to hold up in court, they must know enough about the law to draft a measure that is not unconstitutional. If initiative proponents fail at either of these tasks, then the courts will defeat any measures that the voters do not.

The second stage is the *qualification* stage. After drafting the initiative, the sponsors must form a campaign committee and register with the secretary of state. The state attorney general's office then issues an official title and summary for the initiative. It can also order government agencies to conduct an analysis of the initiative's likely fiscal impact.

To qualify an initiative for the ballot, the California Constitution requires initiative proponents to collect hundreds of thousands of signatures from registered voters. The purpose of this requirement is to limit ballot access to proposals for which there is at least a minimal degree of public interest. The number of signatures required for statutory initiatives is five percent of the votes cast in the last gubernatorial election and for constitutional amendments is eight percent of the votes cast. For elections in the year 2000, the requirement amounted to 419,260 and 670,816 signatures, respectively. In practice, however, proponents actually obtain many more signatures than the minimum required. They do so because the state counts as valid only the signatures of registered voters and because some people sign initiative petitions even though they are not registered. Since people who collect signatures have no easy way to determine who is registered to vote, they cover their potential losses by collecting extra signatures.

The state forces potential initiative proponents to collect signatures quickly. California requires that signatures be collected within 150 days after the committee registers with the secretary of state, and within 131 days of the election. This is no small task. As a result, most recent successful qualification drives relied, at least in part, on paid signature gatherers. Companies that coordinate paid signature-gathering drives hire hundreds of people to go to high traffic areas across the state, usually supermarkets and shopping malls. These people often set up tables with many potential initiatives on them. The companies pay their employees on the basis of the number of signatures they collect. In recent years, initiative proponents have had to pay to signature-gathering companies $1 to $3 per signature (Kimball Petition Management 1997). In sum, groups require either vast sums of money to hire professionals or a standing army of volunteer signature gatherers to have any hope of qualifying their initiative for the California ballot.

The third stage is the *campaign* stage. For most groups using the initiative process, the campaign represents an even higher hurdle than qualification. The most expensive campaign to date in California was the one surrounding Proposition 5 of 1998, the Indian Gaming Initiative. Its supporters spent more than $66 million and opponents spent nearly $26 million, for total expenditures of approximately $92 million. Other expensive campaigns included Proposition 211 of 1996 (Attorney-Client Fee Arrangements, Securities Fraud, Lawsuits), in which proponents and opponents spent $57.2 million, and the insurance measures of 1988 (Propositions 100, 101, 103, 104, and 106), in which proponents and opponents spent more than $84 million on five separate measures.

Numerous factors affect the cost of an initiative campaign. Because the state is so large in population and land area, reaching large segments of the population requires sizable purchases of advertising time on television and radio. Many campaigns also engage heavily in direct mail.

Three factors that affect the cost of winning at the campaign stage are:

- the extent of underlying public support (i.e., whether the campaign seeks to mobilize existing support rather than to change people's opinions),
- the resources of the opposition (i.e., whether the campaign is competitive or noncompetitive), and

- the campaign's purpose (i.e., whether it is intended to pass or defeat an initiative proposition).

We discuss each of these factors in turn.

Creating support that did not previously exist—as initiative proponents must do when they propose a policy that was not previously in the public eye—involves changing people's minds, often a difficult task. Mobilizing existing support requires less effort. It requires reminding the public of an issue with which many people are already familiar, and getting out the vote on Election Day.

A second factor affecting the cost of electoral victory is whether a campaign is competitive or noncompetitive. Running a winning campaign in the absence of vigorous opposition is less expensive than running a competitive campaign. In a one-sided campaign, a campaigner simply needs to make his or her case to the public. In a competitive campaign, that campaigner also needs to respond to the claims, allegations, and attacks of their opponents.

A third factor is whether a campaign is intended to pass a new initiative (i.e., change the status quo policy) or block a proposed initiative (i.e., preserve the status quo). Large expenditures of campaign money are more effective in defeating than in passing initiatives (Lowenstein 1982, Owens and Wade 1986, Gerber 1999). However, Gerber (1999) also shows that while some money is necessary for a ballot measure's passage, proponents of unpopular initiatives routinely fail in their attempts to buy victory. Both of these observations follow from what we know about how voters make decisions when voting on ballot measures. As Bowler and Donovan (1998) show, when voters are uncertain about the likely policy consequences of a ballot proposition, they tend to vote "no." Voters prefer to stick with policies whose consequences they have lived under, which are the policies that continue when initiatives lose, rather than risk voting for a new initiative whose consequences might be very bad. Therefore, spending vast sums of money to defeat an initiative may make voters confused and uncertain enough to vote against it. Convincing voters that an initiative represents an improvement over the known status quo, by contrast, requires more than money. As Lupia (1994) and Lupia and Johnston (2000) show, it also requires the endorsements of well-known public figures and evidence of broad grassroots support.

In sum, citizens and groups who want to use direct initiatives must be capable of overcoming the challenges present in each stage of the initiative process. In recent years, prospective initiative proponents have turned increasingly to a highly professional "initiative industry" to help them clear these hurdles. The professional consultants offer a full range of services, including running polls and focus groups; providing drafting assistance; hiring and managing paid signature gatherers; assisting in fundraising; coordinating advertising, direct mail, and other campaign activities; and assisting with post-election litigation. For those who can afford them, these hired guns are an effective way to get an initiative on the ballot and to give it a chance of winning on Election Day.

WHO TAKES THE INITIATIVE?

Since 1911, only 34 percent of the initiatives that qualified for the California ballot have passed. Of those that passed, the courts overturned many. Given this low rate of success and the extremely high costs of initiative campaigns, why would anyone choose to use direct initiatives? To answer this question, we highlight two common motives of initiative sponsors.

First, the initiative process is the only way for some groups to get the policy they want. Supporters of term limits and certain types of campaign finance reform, for example, wanted policies that state legislators were unwilling to impose on themselves. Other groups advocate policies that the major parties dislike (e.g., open primaries), that cut across existing political cleavages (e.g., bilingual education), that offend important legislative constituencies (e.g., tort reform), or that legislators consider "too hot to handle" (e.g., immigration policy and gay marriage).[2] For these groups, the initiative process is the only way to achieve their policy goals. Moreover, these are the very types of groups the initiative process was initially intended to empower.

Note, however, that since these groups have preferences that conflict with those of government actors, they may face special problems after Election Day. If the same government actors who opposed their policies before the election are later charged with implementing and enforcing these policies, a conflict may arise—*the actors have to choose between pursuing their own policy interests and complying with the policy instructions of a winning initiative.*

A second motivation for initiative users in California is that its initiative process offers a unique benefit—policies that legislatures are not allowed to amend. The Progressive reformers who introduced initiatives and referendums in California deliberately designed the process to circumvent the state legislature. They feared that if the legislature could amend or repeal initiative legislation, it would simply undo any initiatives that it (and its railroad clients) disliked. To this end, California prohibits legislators from amending, revising, rejecting, or otherwise altering laws passed by initiative, except with another popular vote.[3] The state is unique in this regard and this uniqueness very likely contributes to the high frequency of direct initiatives in California.

For a winning initiative's supporters, this prohibition on amendment by the legislature is a great benefit, because it insures its policy gains against shifting political landscapes. From the legislature's perspective, the inability to amend initiative legislation means that it has less incentive to take up policies that are likely to make it to the ballot. It also means that once an initiative passes, its potential to constrain policymakers is great—if government actors choose to comply with the initiative in the first place.

The initiative process in California thus provides policy advocates with a way to circumvent a disagreeable legislature and to protect their policy gains from present and future government actors. As a result, the main consideration for potential initiative proponents is whether these benefits outweigh the initiative process's high costs. We expect, therefore, that the only people who will use initiatives are those who want big policy changes that provide them with enough material or ideological benefits to make their high costs worthwhile.

The requirements of the initiative process, however, will affect what policy changes potential initiative proponents can hope to achieve. Initiative proponents who want to win on Election Day must be able to convince a majority of the electorate to support their initiative. If they want a type of policy that already has broad public support, then they can proceed without having to trade outcomes they want for outcomes that can win. Proponents of policies such as term limits and campaign finance reform clearly had such opportunities.

If, however, a group supports an idea that is less popular, then the decisions they make in the drafting stage are more critical. These groups may have to write measures that water down their own policy preferences in order to make the legislation more acceptable to voters. The need to compromise at the drafting stage drives some potential sponsors away from the initiative process; not getting exactly what they want makes them less able to justify the high cost of waging an initiative campaign. As a result, proponents who want major policy changes and believe they can win without compromise are more likely than others to use the initiative process.

Another way to attract public support is to write vague language that is difficult for opponents to attack. But vagueness opens the door for government actors to reinterpret initiatives they do not like. So, if a proponent's preferences are similar to those of the government actors charged with compliance, using vague language may be a small price to pay for electoral victory. But if important government actors oppose the initiative, as will be the case for groups supporting issues that legislators refused to take up in the past, then *being vague for the purpose of winning the election can backfire when it is time for implementation.*

CONCLUSION

The initiative process in California offers citizens an opportunity to circumvent the legislature and write laws themselves. As this brief review indicates, successful proponents must have substantial resources to collect hundreds of thousands of signatures within a relatively short time and to run a costly, media-dominated campaign. The groups most likely to use direct initiatives are those who have no other way to pass their policy agenda, those who desire a big enough change in policy to justify the process's high costs, and those who have the human and monetary resources that electoral victory requires. Indeed, because the initiative route costs more than what most groups in Sacramento pay for lobbying, it is likely that initiative proponents will request policy changes that extant government actors have proven unwilling to provide. Moreover, the fact that initiative battles are often fought in the form of thirty-second advertisements implies that proponents may also benefit from being able to articulate the benefits of their initiatives quickly, which can induce them to be vague about certain aspects of their policy proposal at the drafting stage.

In short, it is likely that initiative proponents will seek substantial changes in policy that provide a great benefit to a particular constituency (the initiative proponents) against the wishes of at least some current government actors. Such conditions imply that there are likely to be actors in government who will be unfriendly to the initiative after Election Day. We now turn to the ways these actors respond to winning initiatives.

NOTES

1. See Deverell and Sitton 1994 for a discussion of the Progressive era in California and the adoption of initiatives and other Progressive reforms.
2. See Gerber 1999 for a more extensive discussion of interest groups' motivations for using the initiative process.
3. The exception is when the initiative explicitly grants amendment power. By contrast, in all other states, legislators have some power to amend initiative legislation, albeit sometimes only with a supermajority vote and sometimes only after a waiting period of three to five years. See DuBois and Feeney 1992 for a summary of state provisions for post-election legislative amendments.

3

The Politics
of Initiative Compliance

For a winning initiative to affect public policy, government actors must choose to comply with its instructions. Understanding how government actors make these choices is essential for explaining the great variations in what happens to initiatives after they leave the voters' hands. In this chapter, we uncover some of the factors that cause these variations, leading some initiatives to have the policy impact that their authors intended and others to have no policy impact whatsoever.[1]

Our explanation is based, in part, on findings from a model that we designed for the purpose of explaining initiative compliance (Gerber, Lupia, and McCubbins n.d.). The model is technically complex and its details are the types of things in which only social scientists tend to be interested. Since this book is for a broader audience, we will say very little about the model's details in what follows. The model did, however, clarify how we think about what happens to initiatives after they pass. It helped us figure out which of the many claims that people make about initiative compliance are (and are not) consistent with basic facts about state and local politics. Indeed, the model was the vehicle that allowed us to convert the seeming chaos of state and local politics into the relatively simple explanation that follows.

ABOUT OUR EXPLANATION

We base our explanation of initiative compliance on an increasingly common analytic tool called a *principal-agent model*. In a principal-agent model, an actor called the *principal* issues an order and relies on *agents* to carry it out. In some models, the principal is the U.S. Congress and the agents are the federal bureaucracy (see, for example, Kiewiet and McCubbins 1991 and Lupia and McCubbins 1998). In other models, the principals are the voters and the agents are their elected representatives (see, e.g., Lupia 1992, Gerber and Lupia 1995).

Principal-agent models are most helpful in providing insight when principals and agents disagree about what to do and can choose many different ways of pursuing their own agendas. Since politics is full of cases where people disagree, principal-agent models are frequently useful. Indeed, a growing number of political scientists use principal-agent models to explain what happens whenever some actors have to rely on others to achieve the outcomes they desire.

In the principal-agent model from which we draw, the principal is a successful initiative proponent (e.g., the interest groups and voters who are able to pass an initiative). The government actors who must act to carry out the proponent's mandate—often the state legislature and the governor's office—are their agents. Our principal-agent model focuses on critical moments in the policy process at which government actors can thwart an initiative proponent's intentions. Our model produces clear predictions about when government actors will (and will not) "steal" the initiatives and provides the scientific basis of the predictions that follow.

WHAT KINDS OF PEOPLE AFFECT
INITIATIVE COMPLIANCE?

A winning initiative's fate is determined by the actions of two groups of people: initiative proponents and government actors. We use the term initiative *proponents* to refer to the policy advocates who, with the support of organized interest groups, professional consultants, financial supporters, and a sufficient number of voters, can draft, qualify, pass, and defend an initiative against legal challenge.[2] We use the term *government actors* to refer to the individuals and agencies who are responsible for complying with initiatives.

We sometimes find it useful to further distinguish government actors as implementation agents and enforcement agents. *Implementation agents* are people in government responsible for providing official instructions about how to comply with an initiative. *Enforcement agents* are those in government responsible for following those directions. In most cases, different people are assigned implementation and enforcement duties. The state legislature, for example, is often given sole authority to write implementation instructions or to pass implementing legislation regarding a winning initiative. In other cases, the task of writing implementing legislation goes to high-ranking officials in bureaucratic agencies. The governor and state and local bureaucrats are often the actors charged with enforcing implementation instructions. There are also cases in which the line between implementation and enforcement is not so sharply drawn—the same people must decide how to implement an initiative and ensure that it gets enforced.

What initiative proponents and government actors have in common is that most, if not all, of them are motivated, at least in part, by a desire to affect public policy.[3] This is not to say that any or all of these actors have common beliefs about what policy outcomes are best or appropriate. Indeed, there is often substantial disagreement, particularly between initiative proponents and the government actors who prevented the state from enacting, in the past, the same law that the proponents put in their initiative. Such conflicts are important to account for, and are critical to understanding the politics of initiative compliance.

WHAT KINDS OF ACTIONS AFFECT INITIATIVE COMPLIANCE?

Passing an initiative does not guarantee its implementation and enforcement. As is the case with any law passed by a professional legislature, initiatives affect policy outcomes only if government actors choose to comply with the law's policy instructions. To understand these choices, it is useful to think of an initiative's path from Election Day victory to policy change as having two stages: a compliance stage and a sanctioning stage.

Compliance Stage

After Election Day, certain government actors are assigned the duty of responding to a winning initiative. In some cases, initiatives contain precise instructions about how government actors should respond. Consider, for example, the term limits component of 1990's Proposition 140. It specified a maximum of three consecutive terms for members of the State Assembly and two consecutive terms for other elected officials, with a lifetime ban on serving in the same capacity thereafter. Proposition 140's instructions to incumbent legislators and the secretary of state's office, which oversees the conduct of elections, are quite clear.

In other cases, however, winning initiatives provide vague instructions to those charged with implementation. Consider, for example, California's Proposition 209 of 1996. The full text of this famous initiative, which scaled back affirmative action, is as follows:

SEC. 31. (a) The state shall not discriminate against, or grant preferential treatment to, any individual or group on the basis of race, sex, color, ethnicity, or national origin in the operation of public employment, public education, or public contracting.

(b) This section shall apply only to action taken after the section's effective date.

(c) Nothing in this section shall be interpreted as prohibiting bona fide qualifications based on sex which are reasonably necessary to the normal operation of public employment, public education, or public contracting.

(d) Nothing in this section shall be interpreted as invalidating any court order or consent decree which is in force as of the effective date of this section.

(e) Nothing in this section shall be interpreted as prohibiting action which must be taken to establish or maintain eligibility for any federal program, where ineligibility would result in a loss of federal funds to the state.

(f) For the purposes of this section, "state" shall include, but not necessarily be limited to, the state itself, any city, county, city and county, public university system, including the University of California, community college district, school district, special district, or any other political subdivision or governmental instrumentality of or within the state.

(g) The remedies available for violations of this section shall be the same, regardless of the injured party's race, sex, color, ethnicity, or national origin, as are otherwise available for violations of then-existing California antidiscrimination law.

(h) This section shall be self-executing. If any part or parts of this section are found to be in conflict with federal law or the United States Constitution, the section shall be implemented to the maximum extent that federal law and the United States Constitution permit. Any provision held invalid shall be severable from the remaining portions of this section.

After Proposition 209 passed and survived court challenges, state legislators and their counterparts in many government agencies had to spend considerable effort attempting to figure out, and explain to others, what actions regarding protected minorities it allowed. For example, they had to determine whether public entities, such as the University of California, could provide special privileges to students with disadvantaged socioeconomic backgrounds that, though not explicitly racial, were highly correlated with race—even to the point of replicating the consequences of race-based policies. The Proposition itself did not provide an answer and today the answer is still unclear. While Proposition 209 is unusual for its brevity—the full text of most initiatives is thousands of words long—the fact that it requires implementation agents to interpret its meaning gives it something in common with almost all winning initiatives.

In addition to interpretation, most winning initiatives require either the retraining of existing state workers or the development of new bureaucratic agencies. In the case of Proposition 198 of 1996, for example, citizens directed the state to move from a system of closed primaries (where only voters who were registered with a particular party could vote in that party's primary election) to open primaries (where any voter can, in effect, participate in any primary election he or she chooses). After Proposition 198 passed, various implementation agents in the legislature and the secretary of state's office had to write instructions for producing the new ballots and reprogram the new vote counting systems that Proposition 198 required. Since both activities entailed positive costs, implementation agents had to decide whether to make funds available for the changes and if so, how much money to allot. As most winning initiatives force at least one bureaucratic agency to change its past practices, they make the types of decisions just described quite common.

The interpretive and funding decisions that affect a winning initiative's policy impact often appear in *implementing legislation*. In many instances, state legislatures write and pass such legislation. As our case studies reveal, this legislation is critically important; its language affects the extent to which the proponent's vision can change public policy. Indeed, legislatures can and do write implementing legislation that prevents winning initiatives from having any real impact.

Other implementation agents, such as those who work within the state bureaucracy, do not write legislation per se, but they perform equivalent tasks. For example, a school board charged with implementing aspects of an education initiative is likely to have to write special instructions for teachers and administrators in their district. Henceforth, we use the term *implementing legislation* to refer to the broad class of activities where government actors provide instructions about how to respond to a winning initiative. It follows that the job of enforcement agents is to carry out implementing legislation.

An important thing to know about implementation and enforcement agents is that all have choices to make. When developing implementing legislation, for example, implementation agents can choose to comply with the initiative's instructions fully, partially, or not at all. If implementation agents adopt implementing legislation, then compliance is possible and depends on the subsequent reaction of enforcement agents. If, by contrast, all implementation agents refuse to do what is necessary for initiative compliance, then there are no instructions for enforcement agents to act upon and the initiative dies. For example, if an anti-smoking initiative—such as Proposition 99 of 1988—requires the legislature to fund certain educational activities, and the legislature redirects available funds to other purposes, then the educational aims of the initiative can be killed.

A second important thing to know about implementation and enforcement agents is that their actions can be personally costly. The two types of costs that these actors face are *technical costs* and *political costs*. Technical costs include the time and monetary costs of having legislative staff determine how to implement aspects of the initiative, plus the costs of actually establishing, administering, and monitoring mandated programs. Political costs include the difficulty of taking resources away from other programs in order to comply with the initiative. For example, legislative actors may have to promise benefits on other issues to secure the legislative agreement that is necessary for initiative compliance. Note that if the technical and political costs of compliance are high enough, then even government actors who favor the initiative may have a strong incentive (avoiding these costs) not to implement or enforce the initiative fully.

With an understanding of the actors involved in initiative compliance and facts about their circumstances in hand, we can render our first prediction.[4]

Prediction 1: High technical or political costs will correspond to lower levels of compliance

In other words, if government actors decide to implement and enforce an initiative, doing so may be costly to them, above and beyond any consequences they suffer from putting into place an initiative that diverges from their ideal policy. As discussed above, these implementation and enforcement costs may be both technical and political. Since implementation and enforcement costs decrease the net value of complying with an initiative (i.e., they are paid only if there is some level of compliance), we expect compliance to be lower when these costs are high.

Sanctioning Stage

The second stage in the compliance process is a day of reckoning. We include this day of reckoning to represent the following fact: While government actors may have opportunities to thwart initiative proponents' intentions, they do so at some peril. What do implementation and enforcement agents have to worry about? They must worry that an initiative's proponents will sanction them should they discover the government failing to comply with their winning legislation. For example, proponents may have legal standing to sue the state for noncompliance with the initiative. They may also be able to mobilize voters or interest groups to withhold electoral or financial support from uncooperative elected officials when they run for reelection. While such sanctions need not ever be levied, if government actors believe that acting against the electorate's decision can have negative consequences for them, then just the threat of sanctions may be sufficient to induce compliance.[5]

Understanding the power of sanctions, or just the threat of sanctions, leads to our second prediction.

Prediction 2: High sanctions will correspond to higher levels of compliance

One of the most important factors affecting the degree of compliance is the size of the sanction actors might face if they choose to ignore some or all of the initiative's mandate. The larger the sanction, the more important a factor it becomes in the agent's cost-benefit calculation, and the more likely the agent will comply, all else being equal.

Of course, imposing sanctions is not trivial. For proponents to file a lawsuit or pose a credible electoral threat, they require substantial monetary and human resources. A proponent's ability to sanction also depends on its ability to observe the final outcome—after all, proponents can't punish non-compliant agents if they don't know what the agents have done. Because initiative proponents may lack the resources or information needed to wield sanctions, it follows that the likelihood of being sanctioned is as important to an agent's calculations as is the magnitude of the sanction itself.

To understand the likelihood of sanctions for noncompliance, it is useful to consider three factors that make it difficult for initiative proponents to observe compliance.

1. Some initiatives specify a policy goal without describing how to achieve it. When this happens, it can be difficult to determine whether the agent's actions are compliant or noncompliant.
2. Some initiatives specify the steps that agents must take, but are vague about what end results the initiative proponent desires. When this happens, the extent of compliance may be difficult to measure, even if a proponent has good information about government actions.
3. Some initiative proponents lack information about government actions, so even if means and ends are stated clearly, the proponent will be unable to assess compliance. This circumstance is particularly likely when compliance depends on government actions that are difficult for voters to observe and when the groups who sponsored a winning initiative disband (as many do soon after Election Day). In such cases, it may be difficult for proponents to determine the extent to which government actors have followed their orders.

When an initiative's means and ends are clear, when proponents have good information, and when proponents can mobilize the resources needed to carry out sanctions, we should expect the threat of sanctions to influence government actors' implementation and enforcement decisions. If, by contrast, an initiative proponent's ability to observe compliance is sufficiently low, then government actors may have an opportunity to "steal the initiative" with little fear of reprisal from its proponents—even if better-informed proponents would impose large sanctions. This insight leads to our third prediction.

Prediction 3: Ease of observing compliance will correspond to higher levels of compliance

In real politics, sanctions are applied probabilistically—not all transgressions are punished, and when an actor makes an implementation or enforcement decision, he or she does not know for certain whether a failure to comply will be punished. These actors do not make their decisions in the dark, however. It is reasonable to assume that legislators, governors, and other policy actors have *some* idea about how likely they are to be punished for their failure to comply. Their beliefs are related to the ease with which others can observe compliance.

AN IMPORTANT RESULT AND A FINAL PREDICTION

If our representation of the initiative compliance process is accurate, it provides an important insight about initiative compliance:

Full Compliance Result: There is full compliance if and only if implementation and enforcement costs are not prohibitive and one of the following is true:

- All necessary implementation and enforcement agents either favor full compliance over any lower level of compliance or face large expected sanctions.
- Agents who prefer full compliance to the level of compliance that other agents want can restrict the choices of the latter agents in a way that induces them to choose full compliance.

The first bulleted item describes the simplest means by which full compliance occurs—all relevant actors prefer full compliance to any other outcome. Alternatively, if some agents favor full compliance and others do not, full compliance can still be achieved if every actor who favors less-than-full compliance also faces *large expected sanctions*. By this, we mean that the size of the sanction times the probability that initiative proponents can observe noncompliance is large. So, if the expected sanction is greater than the benefits that the actors in question would receive by not complying, the proponents can expect full compliance. Otherwise, initiative proponents should expect government actors to reinterpret or ignore parts of their initiative, and they must settle for an outcome that deviates in some way from their winning proposal.

The second bulleted item describes a more complex means of achieving full compliance. Under certain circumstances, some government actors prefer more compliance than others and have the power to influence others' choices. If those who prefer higher levels of compliance are able to force the others to choose between a level of compliance that brings sufficiently bad things to them, such as big sanctions, and full compliance, then full compliance will be the result.

Consider, for example, a conflict where the legislature prefers greater compliance than the governor. Suppose further that the governor faces large expected sanctions for anything less than full compliance and that the legislature and the governor are the only actors relevant to initiative compliance. If the legislature could get the governor to enforce the high degree of partial compliance that it wants without restricting the governor's actions, it would do so. If it cannot, however, then the legislature can benefit from restricting the governor's choices between full compliance (which will elicit no sanctions) or a level of compliance that the governor would choose if sanctions were not an issue. This action puts the governor in the spotlight and causes him to choose between full compliance and no sanctions or a level of compliance he would have otherwise chosen, accompanied by sanctions. If the sanctions are large enough, the legislature will get what it wants.

In this example, we expect full compliance if the legislature prefers high compliance and the governor disagrees but faces a large expected sanction for partial or noncompliance. Note that if we substitute into the example a legislature that wants low compliance and faces large sanctions, then our expectation—full compliance—does not change. If, however, we substitute a legislature that wants low compliance and faces no sanctions, then the conditions for full compliance are no longer met; such a legislature no longer has an incentive to restrict the governor's actions. In sum, when the conditions in the Full Compliance Result differ from reality, some government actors will block full implementation and enforcement of a winning initiative.

Our fourth and final prediction in this chapter draws on the Full Compliance Result and reveals how the number of actors involved in the compliance stage affects the ultimate extent of initiative compliance. For most winning initiatives, many actors must work together to ensure implementation and enforcement. We know that every additional person who participates will have policy preferences of his or her own. Like the actors described above, many will face technical or political compliance costs and may be subject to sanctions for noncompliance. We also know that once these additional people are part of the compliance process, they have a choice—they can take actions consistent with full compliance, partial compliance, or no compliance at all.

Initiatives regarding the state's education system, for example, require teachers, principals, and members of school boards around the state to join the legislature and the governor in complying with the new law. If teachers are able to reinterpret an initiative or act against it without fear of sanctions, then the initiative's effect on policy in the classroom will be just as it would have been had the initiative failed at the polls (this example foreshadows our analysis of Proposition 227 in Chapter 13). When some classrooms comply with the initiative while others do not, statewide compliance—the type of compliance in which we are most interested—can be no more than partial.

Since the number of people involved in implementation and enforcement varies from initiative to initiative, our final prediction clarifies the relationship between the extent of initiative compliance and the number of government actors that full compliance requires. To state that prediction, we need one additional definition.

When many actors can affect initiative compliance, it can be complicated to think about what will happen. To simplify matters, we define a situation that we regard as "normal conditions" for most initiatives that pass in California. Under normal conditions, every additional agent need not prefer full compliance to any other outcome, nor are these agents necessarily subject to large sanctions for noncompliance. Indeed, the probability that any particular government actor supports full compliance in any particular real-world circumstance is difficult to guess in advance. Therefore, when we analyze initiative compliance, it is helpful to make the least restrictive assumption about the preferences in question. The less restrictive the assumptions we make, the broader the analysis's applicability. So we assume that under normal conditions, the probability that any randomly selected government actor either favors full compliance or faces large sanctions is below 100 percent—it can be any other amount from 0 to 99.99 percent. Put another way, we assume that under normal conditions there is at least some chance that each additional government actor will most prefer some outcome other than full compliance and will not be subject to large sanctions for acting on his or her preferences. This assumption is almost certainly true for most real-world initiatives.

Such "normal conditions" produce the following result.

Prediction 4: *Under normal conditions, as the number of people required for full compliance increases, the likelihood of full compliance goes to zero*

In other words, when numerous actors are required to implement and enforce an initiative, the opportunities for actors to reinterpret or ignore the initiative's instructions increase and the likelihood that *all* actors will comply with the initiative becomes small. We therefore expect that as the number of actors involved increases, the level of compliance will be lower.

Our final prediction has important implications. It states that even if many government actors are likely to favor full compliance, adding enough actors to the process, under normal conditions, ensures that full compliance will not occur. In other words, we do not have to know much about the government actors in question to know that if implementation and enforcement require the participation of many people, then full compliance is very unlikely.

Taken together, our predictions imply that under normal conditions the preferences of government actors limit the extent to which the preferences of initiative proponents determine an initiative's policy effect. That is,

- when multiple actors are required to implement and enforce an initiative under normal conditions,
- in the absence of sanctions for *all* government actors involved in implementation and enforcement,
- or in the absence of a legislature, executive, and bureaucracy that all fully support full compliance,

the preferences of initiative proponents will be at least partially displaced by the preferences of government actors.

By this claim, we do not mean to say that the preferences of the initiative proponents are irrelevant to an initiative's ultimate policy effect or that winning initiatives never have the policy effect that their proponents' envision. We do mean to say, however, that without a heavy dose of initiative supporters or high sanctions among the ranks of those charged with implementation and enforcement, someone, somewhere, will reinterpret or reject the voters' mandate. When we recall the fact that people are likely to use the initiative process when they want outcomes that government actors have chosen not to provide in the past, then we realize just how much the deck is stacked against full compliance. Indeed, under normal conditions, government actors will steal the initiatives.

NOTES

1. Throughout the book, we focus on initiatives that are not being challenged in the courts or that have been found constitutional after a challenge. In theory, we could also examine the judicial review of winning initiatives. Several factors, however, dissuaded us from taking that path. First, there is a great deal of debate in the legal community over how courts decide these cases—whether judges are motivated by policy preferences, by their strict interpretation of the constitution, or by a desire for consistency with previous decisions—all of which imply different research strategies. Rather than take a position in this debate, we leave these questions to legal scholars. Second and perhaps more important, we believe that understanding the implementation and en-

forcement decisions of noncourt actors is critical, independent of what the courts do. This aspect of the initiative process is not well studied and increases the potential value of the work we describe herein.

2. There is, of course, the prior question of what type of interests can mobilize such support. See Gerber 1999 for an in-depth analysis of this question. For the purpose at hand, we simply recognize that such interests exist and focus on the extent to which government actors comply with the initiatives they pass.

3. Note that our explanation of the politics of initiative compliance does not depend on any particular assumption about the origin of actor preferences. It does not matter, for example, whether a legislature's preferences result from individual legislators' ideologies, party platforms, constituency pressures, or reelection considerations and whether the governor's preferences derive from election promises, career ambitions, or ideology. All that we require is that implementation and enforcement agents are concerned with more than just empty posturing; for our explanation to be descriptive of reality, the legislature and the governor must have at least some concern with the policy consequences of their actions.

4. We offer our predictions with the caveat "all else constant." In our model, the effects of factors such as costs are contingent on other factors. The predictions we offer here provide a rough, but intuitive, idea of what we found in a more rigorous technical analysis of our model.

5. The difference between the sanctions we describe here and the technical and political costs we described earlier is that the technical and political costs of implementation and enforcement are the costs government actors face if they choose to comply with an initiative. Sanctions, by contrast, are the costs that government actors face for choosing not to comply. In some cases, then, government actors may face costs regardless of how they react to an initiative and may be forced to choose the lesser of two evils.

4

Methods

In the chapters that follow, we use case studies of winning initiatives to further reveal the politics of initiative compliance. In this brief chapter, we describe why we chose the case study method and how we selected our cases.

WHY CASE STUDIES?

We can use numerous analytic approaches to examine initiative compliance. One common approach in political science is to find a simple statistical measure of initiative compliance that is comparable across all of the many policy areas that initiatives cover. With such a measure in hand, we could test general hypotheses about how factors such as compliance costs and sanctions affect winning initiatives. But no such measure of initiative compliance exists.

For any initiative, compliance can involve spending certain amounts of money on special activities, implementing new economic or social regulations, or taking any one of a number of actions in an attempt to achieve particular levels of performance. For some initiatives, the best measure of compliance would enumerate all of these factors. For other initiatives, measuring just one of the factors, such as spending, would be sufficient. Since compliance can be measured in so many different ways, any attempt to put all of these factors into a simple statistical measure would throw away valuable information about the real politics of initiative compliance.

We chose, therefore, to base our examination of initiative compliance on a detailed understanding of the political circumstances in which government actors made compliance decisions about a select number of initiatives. This is why we chose the case study method.

HOW WE CHOSE CASES TO STUDY

Our goal in selecting cases was to collect a set of examples that would allow us to differentiate the initiatives that government actors implement from the initiatives that they ignore. Therefore, we collected data for all winning initiatives in California that were not entirely invalidated by the courts, from 1979 to 1998. Table 4.1 shows some of the data we collected. Reading from left to right, Table 4.1's columns provide information on:

- the winning initiative's number,
- the year in which the initiative was passed,

(*text continued on p. 31*)

Table 4.1   Relevant Variables for Winning Initiatives, 1979–1998

Prop	Year	Sanction Size		# Actors/ Observability	Compliance Costs
		Net Support (1998 $)	*Vote Margin*	*Agents* [a]	*LAO cost estimate* [b]
4	**1979**	**$4,005,105**	**45.2**	**L, LG**	**Unknown**
12	1982	4,281,184	4.3	G	None
24	1984	−323,962	5.0	L	$58.4 million
37	1984	−3,570,258	15.0	L, S	$788.5 million/yr revenue increase
38	1984	111,598	38.2	G	Trivial
51	1986	−1,079,774	22.7	C	Potentially several million dollars in annual savings
62	1986	2,015,614	13.9	LG	Unknown revenue losses
63	**1986**	**19,627**	**42.8**	**L**	**None**
65	1986	−4,588,672	23.2	G, S, LG	$1.5 million/yr

Table 4.1 Relevant Variables for Winning Initiatives, 1979–1998 (*continued*)

Prop	Year	Sanction Size		# Actors/ Observability	Compliance Costs
		Net Support (1998 $)	Vote Margin	Agents [a]	LAO cost estimate [b]
68	1988	−75,491	5.0	L, S	$13.7 million/yr
70	1988	1,487,624	27.2	G, S, LG	$87.3 million/yr
73	1988	−972,682	14.5	None	$900,000/yr savings
96	1988	474,201	22.5	C, S, LG	Up to $1.3 million/yr
97	**1988**	**2,236,009**	**6.5**	**G, S**	**$14 million/yr**
98	1988	7,075,082	1.3	L, S, LG	At least $290 million/yr
99	**1988**	**-26,132,878**	**15.4**	**L, S**	**Additional annual revenues of several hundred million dollars**
103	1988	−17,401,704	2.1	C, S,	$13–20 million
105	1988	545,010	7.8	S	$700,000/yr
115	1990	2,228,911	12.3	C	Unknown
116	**1990**	**2,058,227**	**5.9**	**S, LG**	**$218 million/yr**
117	1990	1,003,012	4.4	S, LG	$37 million/yr
132	1990	703,636	1.0	S	Minimal
139	1990	1,316,248	7.3	S, LG	Unknown savings
140	**1990**	**1,479,339**	**3.9**	**L**	**$85 million/yr**
162	1992	2,330,077	1.7	S	$1–3 million/yr savings
163	1992	2,106,601	30.6	None	Revenue losses of at least $300 million/yr
164	1992	1,163,258	24.7	S	None
184	**1994**	**1,602,389**	**40.3**	**C, LG**	**None**
187	1994	−2,542,830	17.2	S, LG	Potential savings of $216 million/yr; potential costs of $16 billion/yr
198	**1996**	**915,621**	**17.6**	**S, LG**	**Minor savings**
208	1996	1,052,010	20.5	S, LG	Up to $4 million/yr
209	1996	1,826,408	8.6	S, LG	Potential savings of $130 million/yr

(*continued*)

Table 4.1   Relevant Variables for Winning Initiatives, 1979–1998 (*continued*)

Prop	Year	Sanction Size		# Actors/ Observability	Compliance Costs
		Net Support (1998 $)	*Vote Margin*	*Agents* [a]	*LAO cost estimate* [b]
210	1996	887,241	21.6	S	$287 million/yr
213	1996	775,544	49.5	C	$5.2 million/yr
215	1996	1,365,253	10.5	None	None
218	1996	1,547,435	11.7	C, LG	At least $104 million/yr
225	1998	401,648	5.1	L, C	Minor
227	**1998**	**-3,623,431**	**20.7**	**S, LG**	**$50 million/yr**

[a] L = Legislature; G = Governor; S = other state officials, agencies, or bodies; C = courts; LG = local government entities or officials.

[b] LAO estimates presented in the table sometimes do not capture the certainty or potential variation of estimates. More detailed descriptions are given in the pages following this table.

Notes:

Net Support is the difference between campaign receipts of committees supporting the initiative and receipts of committees opposing the initiative (in constant 1998 dollars). A negative number indicates that opponents outspent proponents.

Vote Margin is the difference between those voting for and those voting against a proposition, divided by the total number of people voting in the election.

Agents is those persons or bodies specifically delegated compliance responsibilities in the text of the initiative.

LAO cost estimate is the estimated costs or savings expected from compliance of the initiative.

Bold type highlights the propositions included in our case studies.

Sources:

Vote Margin: California Secretary of State. 1979–1998. *Statement of Vote.*

Net Support: California Fair Political Practices Commission, campaign disclosure reports 1979–1990; California Secretary of State, campaign disclosure reports, 1992–1998. Measured as total receipts of supporting committees in real 1998 dollars.[1] Deflator: 1979–1997 is California CPI for all urban consumers, California Dept. of Finance web page, *http://www.dof.ca.gov/.*

Agents, LAO cost estimate: California Secretary of State. 1979–1998. Ballot Pamphlet.

[1]Period covered, by year: for 1982–86, since there is no indication of dates covered, we assume it is the whole period; 1979 is through 1/3/80; 1988 primary is through 6/30/88; 1988 general is through 12/31/88; 1990 primary is through 6/30/90; 1990 general is through 12/31/90; 1992 general is through 10/17/92; 1994 primary and general (published 7/95) doesn't indicate; 1996 primary and general is through 6/30/96; 1998 primary, from Secretary of State's web site (*www.ss.ca.gov*), is total campaign contributions received in support through 3/17/98, plus late contributions to committees formed primarily to support 225 or 227 (through 6/2/98).

- whether it was passed in a general (G), primary (P), or special (S) election,
- net financial support (the difference between the contributions received by the proponent's and opponent's campaigns),
- vote margin (the difference between the percentage of voters who voted for the initiative and the percentage who voted against it),
- the types of government agents involved (about which we will say more below), and
- the Legislative Analyst Office's estimate of the initiative's fiscal impact.

As you can see, we gathered data that would help us estimate the factors that Chapter 3 suggested would be important: data about sanctions, the number of agents involved in implementation and enforcement, and the technical and political costs of compliance. Gathering such data was not simple because each of these factors is hard to observe. Sanctions, the number of agents required for compliance, and political costs tend not to be objective, measurable characteristics of the political environment; they often depend on government actors' expectations and beliefs, as well as on case-specific or other intangible factors. Therefore, to satisfy our goal, we had to make decisions about what the available data implied about the sanctions, costs, and number of agents that we expected would produce different levels of compliance across examples. The decisions we made are as follows.

We measure the size of the sanction that an initiative's supporters can impose using two kinds of data on the relative strength of the initiative's supporters and opponents. The first kind of data we use is the *vote margin*— the difference between the percentage of voters in favor of the proposition and the percentage opposed to it. We reason that the larger the net electoral support for a measure, the greater the potential sanction faced by government actors who attempt to defy the initiative, if all else is constant. Note that many voters do not vote on every proposition on the ballot in a given year, so we calculate vote margin from the percentage *of all voters who voted in the given election* that supported and opposed each measure, then took the difference between these figures. We believe that this figure presents a more accurate measure of the likely electoral ramifications of noncompliance than the more commonly reported yes/no percentages, which are the percentage *of those who voted on the particular measure*. Interestingly, more than one-third of all the initiatives in our sample were supported by fewer than half of all voters who voted in the election. Note that in our case studies, we complement the vote margin statistic given above with the more conventional statistic—we report the percentage voting yes of those who voted on the initiative.

The second kind of data we use is *net financial support*—the difference between what supporters and opponents raised during the initiative campaign. We reason that the greater this difference, the greater is the proponent's willingness (to spend monetary resources) and ability (having no wealthy opponent to help government actors fight sanctions later on) to mobilize additional resources to sanction government actors for noncompliance after the election. If, for example, proponents and opponents either both spend a lot of money or both spend nothing, we should not expect proponents to impose sanctions easily.

To measure the number of government actors involved in the compliance process, we record the identity of the agents to whom each initiative explicitly delegates compliance responsibilities. These include the legislature (L), the governor (G), other state officials, agencies, or bodies (S), the courts (C), and local government entities or officials (LG). Our reasoning here is that the greater the number of government actors involved in compliance, the less likely is full compliance. We also posit that the involvement of more actor types makes it harder for proponents to observe compliance. Because general measures of the ease of observing compliance are difficult to acquire, we use the information on agent types when discussing compliance observability in this chapter. In the case studies, we combine these measures with case-specific data (e.g., the types of activities that compliance requires) to clarify the relationship between observability and compliance.

We measure government actors' technical and political compliance costs by employing the Legislative Analyst Office's estimate of the initiative's fiscal impact. We reason that the higher the cost of an initiative in terms of its fiscal impact on the state's budget, the greater the political trade-offs that government actors must make to comply with the initiative. These costs apply equally to measures that involve a negative budgetary impact (i.e., measures that increase spending or reduce revenues) and a positive budgetary impact (i.e., measures that reduce spending or increase revenues). Thus, for initiatives that increase spending on new programs, reduce spending on existing programs, lower revenues, or raise taxes, people who benefited from the taxing and spending patterns before the initiative now face the risk that government actors will reallocate their piece of the fiscal pie to pay for initiative compliance. The greater the budgetary impact, the greater the threat to current recipients of government services, and the more painful the political decisions that government actors will have to make. In the case studies, we also introduce case-specific information on the technical costs of each initiative (e.g., whether the initiative required establishing a new program or regulatory agency).

Given these data, our next step was to choose cases for study. It was tempting to look only at cases where measuring and observing factors relevant to compliance is relatively easy. However, doing so would have created a serious problem. If we only analyze initiatives for which observing compliance is relatively easy, we risk biasing our study in favor of observing compliance. Such bias could lead us to conclude that compliance is more frequent and complete than it actually is. Therefore, we wanted to include in our analysis some initiatives for which observing compliance is difficult, but data are nevertheless available. Fortunately, such cases exist.

The bold font rows in Table 4.1 denote the cases we selected. As you can see, these cases differ substantially in net financial support, vote margin, agent types, and LAO cost estimate. We reasoned that because these cases contain substantial variation in the factors that we predict will affect compliance, they would give us substantial variability in the extent of compliance observed. In addition, we chose to do an extensive case study of 1978's Proposition 13, California's most famous initiative.

Now we turn to the cases. We present the cases in roughly chronological order. The exception is that we save the two most detailed case studies, those of Proposition 4 (1979) and Proposition 13 (1978), for last.

In each of the cases, we describe the real politics that led the ten initiatives we study to have such different policy effects. Our Chapter 3 discussion of the politics of initiative compliance guides all of our examinations. In particular, the factors named in our four predictions and our Full Compliance Result appear repeatedly as the key influences on government actors at critical moments in the compliance process. We hope that each successive case provides you with a way to see how these factors actually work and, more important, a greater understanding of when government actors can steal the initiative.

5

Proposition 63 of 1986, English Only

BACKGROUND

In 1986, California voters passed Proposition 63, also known as the *English Only Initiative*. Proposition 63 "made English the state's official language, and required the legislature and officials to take necessary steps to 'preserve and strengthen it'" (California Secretary of State 1996).

A committee called the California English Campaign coordinated Proposition 63's campaign. The committee's leading spokesmen were its chairman Stanley Diamond and former U.S. Senator S. I. Hayakawa. The proponents argued that a common language would unify California's increasingly diverse population and encourage assimilation of non-English speaking immigrants. The committee gathered more than 1 million signatures to qualify the measure for the ballot, using largely volunteer signature gatherers.

Proposition 63 was opposed by a coalition of civil rights groups and related organizations representing Latinos, Asian Americans, and other ethnic and language minorities. Of these organizations, the most visible was the American Civil Liberties Union. Most of the state's Democratic political establishment, including San Francisco Mayor Dianne Feinstein, State Senator Art Torres, and Assembly Speaker Willie Brown, joined in opposing Proposition 63. Opponents argued that the measure was thinly veiled racism that was intended to alienate recent immigrants and nonnative speakers.

EXPECTATIONS

Proposition 63 fails to meet the requirements stated in Chapter 3's Full Compliance Result. Of the people who voted on Proposition 63, 73.2 percent voted yes, signaling the potential for significant electoral sanctions if state policymakers chose not to comply. However, the language of the initiative was so vague that proponents could easily mistake compliance for noncompliance. The initiative instructed state officials to "make English the state's official language." It did not, however, provide specific instructions about how to do so. Melissa Warren, assistant media director for the secretary of state, put it best: "I don't know if anyone knows what Proposition 63 actually means. It was a masterpiece of vagueness" (Braun 1987).

Proposition 63 also promised to impose high technical and political costs on any actor who attempted to implement it. Some of its broad directives, such as "ensuring that immigrants are taught English as quickly as possible (except as required by federal law)," were quite controversial. Moreover, depending on how the provision was interpreted, it could require millions of dollars for new programs, causing increased political tension in subsequent state budget negotiations.

Since many government actors who were asked to implement the measure were against it (in particular, the Democrats who controlled the state assembly); since vague language made compliance difficult to observe and, hence, made expected sanctions for noncompliance low; and since compliance costs were high, Proposition 63 had the makings of a winning initiative that government actors would ignore.

WHAT HAPPENED

Proposition 63 was, in fact, all but ignored by state officials. Most officials were content to postpone any action until the initiative surfaced in the courts (Ingram 1986). Governor Deukmejian, a Republican, predicted that "many, many lawsuits" would be filed and refused to say if or how he would enforce the initiative (Ingram 1986). Assembly Speaker Willie Brown (D-San Francisco) and Senate President Pro Tempore David Roberti (D-Los

Angeles) also opposed Proposition 63 and made clear that its spirit would not live in law (Ingram 1986).

Periodically, state officials tried to realize parts of the initiative. State Senator Art Torres (D-Los Angeles), for example, proposed a bill that authorized approximately $5.5 million to teach English to the functionally illiterate and to adults who spoke foreign languages. Although he was an outspoken critic of Proposition 63, Torres presented his bill as an attempt to implement one of its provisions. Three years later, Assemblyman Tom McClintock (R-Thousand Oaks) proposed a bill that would prohibit state and local governments from providing most nonvital services in languages other than English. Though the Torres and McClintock bills differed in their intent, they shared a common fate—both failed.

Attorney General John Van de Kamp reacted in a different way: with defiance. In the best-known incident involving Proposition 63, California English Campaign chair Stanley Diamond filed a complaint with Van de Kamp in 1987, requesting legal action to force the state to comply with the initiative. Diamond was incensed over San Francisco's continued use of trilingual election materials (Spanish, Chinese, and English), as well as provision, on request, of Spanish translations in San Marcos and Carlsbad. While he did not seek nullification of the results of any election run with such materials, he did want to compel the state to implement and enforce the initiative in the future.

Van de Kamp issued a nonbinding research memorandum defending the use of voting materials in non-English languages in all three locations (*San Diego Union-Tribune* 1987). Van de Kamp argued that as he read the law, Proposition 63 required only that official publications be printed and made available in English—as opposed to requiring that such materials be made available in English only. This is not the interpretation that Diamond and his followers had in mind. When Proposition 63's supporters complained about his interpretation, Van de Kamp quipped, "If that was what was intended, it was not written into the constitutional text adopted by voters" (Carson 1987).

Other officials went beyond Van de Kamp's reinterpretation of Proposition 63. In a less publicized case the same year, Assemblyman Elihu Harris (D-Oakland) offered a bill that would have emasculated citizens' power to sue for the enforcement of the initiative's provisions (Gilliam 1987). Harris's bill permitted suits only in cases of laws passed after Proposition 63's approval, and even then, only within 120 days of the proposition's enactment. Harris's bill would have had the effect of protecting long-standing non-English programs, like bilingual education, from legal challenge.

The State Assembly debated Harris's bill and the discussion was intense (Gilliam 1987). At first, Harris had plenty of Democratic support. Then Frank Hill, a Republican assemblyman from Whittier, threatened to mail 200,000 leaflets informing voters of the Democrats' support for Harris's bill.

Whether Hill's move caused what happened next is unclear, but when the bill came to a vote, Harris urged his fellow Democrats to abstain, resulting in a final vote of 26 to 4 against the bill, with 50 abstentions.

The flight to abstention in this case underscores the importance of sanctions for understanding initiative compliance. It shows how fear of electoral sanctions thwarted a flagrant attempt to overturn Proposition 63's Election Day victory. Indeed, Harris' bill attempted to overturn one of Proposition 63's less ambiguous components—the part that gave voters standing to sue to enforce its provisions. It appears that when Hill threatened to inform voters about Harris's attempt to revoke their legal standing, Harris and his supporters recognized the looming threat of sanctions and backed down. This legislative turnaround not withstanding, Proposition 63 has never been seriously implemented.

6

Proposition 97 of 1988, Cal/OSHA

BACKGROUND

In the 1988 general election, voters passed Proposition 97, the state Occupational Safety and Health Plan. Proposition 97 required the state to reinstate its workplace safety program, Cal/OSHA (the California Occupational Safety and Health Act).

Governor George Deukmejian had discontinued Cal/OSHA the year before. Under federal law, states must either be part of the federal OSHA program or operate their own OSHA program, with the proviso that state programs must be approved by the federal government and at least as rigorous as the federal OSHA. Governor Deukmejian's decision was, therefore, part of a plan to transfer responsibility and expenses for workplace safety from his state budget to the federal treasury in Washington. Soon after Governor Deukmejian discontinued the state program, the federal program began to set up operations in California.

The consensus at the time, however, was that Cal/OSHA was far more rigorous and stringent in its monitoring and enforcement of workplace safety than was the federal program. In the next election, voters agreed by passing Proposition 97 and ordering the state to resurrect Cal/OSHA. It also instructed that the budget bill include "amounts sufficient to fully carry out the purposes and provisions of the state plan in this code in a manner which assures that the risk of industrial injury will be minimized" (California Secretary of State 1988, p. 75).

EXPECTATIONS

Governor Deukmejian opposed Proposition 97. He was an outspoken critic of the old Cal/OSHA, personally ordered the program's discontinuation, formed a campaign committee to oppose the measure, and contributed $2000 to the opposing campaign. The Democratic legislature, with its strong support from organized labor, favored the initiative. Most of the $1.5 million raised by Proposition 97's proponents came from labor and public employees unions, Democratic Party organizations, and Democratic candidates and officeholders. Therefore, strictly on the basis of preferences, we would expect the legislature to favor implementation of Proposition 97 and the governor to oppose enforcement.

As highlighted in Chapter 3, however, government actors' preferences are not the only factors that affect initiative compliance. Expected sanctions that can force the hand of noncompliant government actors also play a role. Governor Deukmejian had good reason to believe that he would be subject to sanctions if he ignored Proposition 97. Some segments of the public were highly mobilized on the issue and were offended that the governor had closed down the original Cal/OSHA. More important from Deukmejian's perspective, support for Cal/OSHA from voters in his own Republican party was also substantial, with many self-identified Republicans indicating likely support for Proposition 97 in the Field Poll's final preelection survey (Field Institute 1988). Interest groups, especially labor unions, were also highly mobilized and displayed their ability to raise money for this issue in their financing of the "Yes on 97" campaign. If the governor openly defied the instructions in Proposition 97 by delaying or refusing to institute a new Cal/OSHA, he would make many enemies.

In addition to high sanctions making compliance likely, some parts of the initiative offered precise instructions about how to comply. Specifically, the initiative required funding for the reinstituted program to be at its 1987 levels. Monitoring whether these funds were allocated and spent on the reinstituted program would be relatively easy.

Not all aspects of the initiative, however, were so precise. In particular, it would be difficult for Proposition 97's proponents to monitor the government's compliance with the more performance-based components of the mandate (i.e., ensuring workplace safety). The initiative specified the means for reinstating Cal/OSHA, but it was vague about the ends that reinstatement was supposed to achieve.

We therefore expect the legislature and the governor to comply with the financing mandate contained in the initiative. To the extent that the governor was able to exert discretion, however, it would be over the program's performance-based components.

WHAT HAPPENED

Following the election, Governor Deukmejian immediately stated that he would abide by the voters' decision and revive Cal/OSHA. Within a month, he reestablished the program in compliance with Proposition 97. As Figure 6.1 shows, budget allocations for "Section 4" spending, which includes Cal/OSHA, were returned to pre-1987 levels.

Even so, enforcement of the restored program was halfhearted, if not deliberately obstructionist. For example, the reconstituted agency had fewer offices than did its predecessor (Baker 1990). And a little more than a year after the restoration, a review of the agency found that the program had fewer employees and was making 24 percent fewer inspections than it had in 1987 (Weinstein 1988). Figure 6.2 reports the number of scheduled inspec-

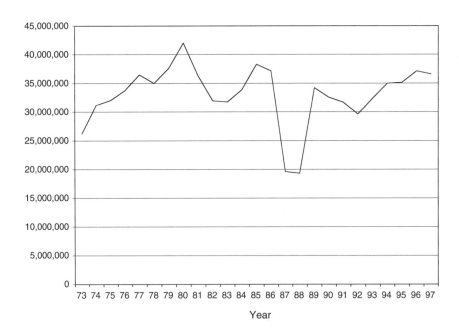

Figure 6.1   Section 4 Spending, 1982–1984 Dollars

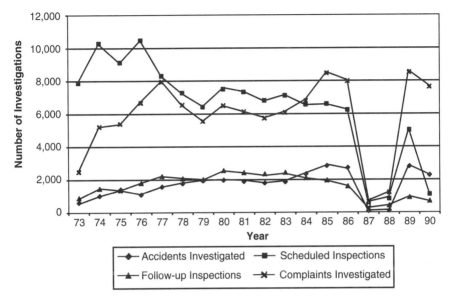

Figure 6.2 Performance Measures for Cal/OSHA

tions, follow-up inspections, complaints investigated, and accidents investigated by Cal/OSHA.

Critics charged Governor Deukmejian with sabotaging the new program, noting that two of the top people he appointed to *restore* Cal/OSHA had signed official arguments *against* Proposition 97. This included the head of the agency, whom former Assemblyman Tom Hayden referred to as "not even a caretaker [of Cal/OSHA], but a mortician" (Baker 1990).

At a legislative hearing investigating the new Cal/OSHA's compliance with Proposition 97, Los Angeles County District Attorney Ira Reiner noted that the Administration "seems to be trying to accomplish indirectly [sabotaging Cal/OSHA] what they could not accomplish directly" (Baker 1990). Perhaps the most compelling evidence of this stance is that the newly constituted agency scheduled substantially fewer initial inspections and made far fewer follow-up inspections than did its predecessor. It did, however, continue to respond to complaints and to investigate accidents at approximately the same rate as the pre-Proposition 97 agency. Thus, by exerting discretion over appointments to the reinstituted agency, the governor was able to comply with the letter of the initiative, yet still direct policy in a way that circumvented (at least in part) its proponents' intent and more closely reflected his own preferences. For the remainder of Governor Deukmejian's term, the effect of Proposition 97 was less than its proponents had envisioned.

7

Proposition 99 of 1988, Tobacco Tax

BACKGROUND

To reduce smoking and other tobacco use, California voters passed Proposition 99 in 1988. The initiative raised the state cigarette tax by 25 cents per pack and imposed a similar tax on other tobacco products. It also contained a strict formula that directed these new tax revenues into six accounts contained within the new Cigarette and Tobacco Products Surtax Fund (CTPSF). The six accounts, their claims on the tobacco surtax revenue, and their purposes (as described in the initiative) are as follows:

1. *Health Education Account* (20 percent): school and community education programs to prevent and reduce tobacco use, mainly among children.
2. *Hospital Services Account* (35 percent): treatment of the poor (payment to hospitals).
3. *Physician Services Account* (10 percent): treatment of the poor (payment to physicians).
4. *Research Account* (5 percent): tobacco-related disease research.

5. *Public Resources Account* (5 percent): protection of fish, waterfowl, and wildlife habitat; enhancement of state and local parks.
6. *Unallocated Account* (25 percent): any purpose specified in the other five accounts.

Proposition 99 specified that money in each account was to be used only for the purposes associated with that account. It allowed the legislature to amend the measure, but only with a four-fifths vote in both chambers, and only if the amendment was consistent with the initiative's purposes.

The tobacco industry spent $21.2 million in an attempt to defeat Proposition 99 (California Fair Political Practices Commission 1988). Though the initiative's supporters spent far less ($1.8 million), Proposition 99 prevailed by winning 58.2 percent of the vote.

EXPECTATIONS

Proposition 99 failed to meet the requirements listed in the Full Compliance Result. On the one hand, the initiative's language was clear and specific, and it mandated easily observable activities by the legislature (i.e., appropriating revenues to designated activities) and state bureaucracy (i.e., collecting new tobacco taxes, administering designated programs). The initiative received substantial voter support (58.2 percent), signaling the possibility of electoral sanctions for noncompliance. And technical costs were low, requiring minimal new administrative support for some new, but fully funded, programs.[1] Thus, while some legislators and the governor were opposed to the measure, we would expect the threat of sanctions to encourage compliance.

On the other hand, however, one major factor stood in the way of full implementation and enforcement of Proposition 99. Tobacco companies made it clear that they could impose significant political costs on compliant politicians by discontinuing campaign contributions. Many California lawmakers received substantial campaign contributions from the tobacco industry. The industry's average campaign contribution to senators was $10,837, and Governor George Deukmejian received $59,250 in tobacco industry contributions between 1982 and 1988.[2] Many California politicians risked the loss of a reliable source of campaign contributions if they took actions consistent with Proposition 99's provisions.

The tobacco industry was particularly concerned about two components of Proposition 99: Its tax hike and its education programs. Both were intended to reduce smoking. Therefore, both threatened consumer demand for tobacco products and, hence, industry profits.

The tobacco lobby could hardly hope to prevent merchants from collecting the new tax, but it could put pressure on legislators and the governor to withhold full funding from the education programs. Since enabling legislation was required for any expenditure to be made from new tobacco tax monies, and (at least tacit) compliance by the governor was required for new programs to be enforced, the tobacco industry could easily target these activities. There was thus considerable potential for noncompliance with parts of Proposition 99.

WHAT HAPPENED

Compliance with Proposition 99 has indeed been partial. The state quickly established the CTPSF and its six accounts, and the tax was levied in exactly the way Proposition 99 instructed. Nevertheless, expenditures from those six accounts have not gone according to plan. The Health Education Account (HEA) and the Research Account (RA), the accounts charged with anti-smoking education, were the main victims.

In 1989, the legislature passed and Governor Deukmejian signed AB 75. This bill diverted over $28 million from Proposition 99's education and research programs between 1989 and 1991 to pay for medical care for the poor.[3] The Legislative Counsel's advice that the diversion violated Proposition 99 and the California Constitution went unheeded.[4]

Excerpts from an internal Tobacco Institute memo, dated April 11, 1990, suggest that the tobacco industry influenced this move:[5]

> Even before Proposition 99 was adopted, plans were in place to continue the fight in the event of passage. After Proposition 99 was approved, a suit was filed attacking its validity. At the same time as the legal action was underway, The Institute initiated a plan to effect a redistribution of Proposition 99 funds. Of these funds, $176 million was to be allocated to anti-smoking 'health education' under the direction of the Department of Health Services. Anti-tobacco proponents wanted virtually every penny of that $176 million spent on tobacco 'education' through the media. Despite Herculean efforts, our goal of completely eliminating the media education was not met. But through our work, the media component was sliced to $14.3 million for fiscal year 1989–90. Another $14.3 million is allocated for fiscal year 1990–91, for a total to date of $28.6 million....
>
> To effect our political strategies of encouraging the Governor and the Legislature to intercede against the advertisements, the State Activities Division is consulting with political and media experts from every possible background.... the Governor [Deukmejian] is made uncomfortable by the campaign.... Assembly Speaker [Willie] Brown, Senate President [David] Roberti and other key legislative leaders have been approached....

The same memo suggests that the California Medical Association also wished to redirect Proposition 99's education funds.

> The industry has been approached by …physician groups, expressing an interest in working with us so that *they* may receive monies that are currently earmarked to the media 'education' campaign. These avenues continue to be explored with the …California Medical Association [emphasis added].

Diversion of Proposition 99 funds continued during Pete Wilson's term as Governor and again despite the Legislative Counsel's advice to the contrary (Opinion No. 5360). In 1991, Governor Wilson signed AB 99, which diverted $112.7 million from education and research programs between 1991 and 1994 to pay for medical care for the poor. In January 1992, the state suspended its much-touted anti-smoking media campaign altogether (Weintraub 1992).

At the time, Governor Wilson argued that the state needed CTPSF money to help cope with its budget crisis (Traitel 1992). State Health Director Molly Joel Coye agreed, arguing that in a fiscal environment necessitating $300 million in cuts in medical services, "temporarily redirecting" Proposition 99 monies was "necessary and fair" (Coye 1992). Echoing Coye, Steven M. Thompson, a lobbyist for the California Medical Association, argued that the diversions were just part of the "politics of scarcity" (Coye 1992). He claimed that the diversions furthered the purposes of Proposition 99's Health Education Account because doctors in the state's Child Health Disabilities Prevention (CHDP) Program, which funds medical care for low-income kids, were required to speak with children and their parents about the dangers of smoking.

Proposition 99's supporters took the Wilson administration to court over its diversions of the initiative's revenues. In the 1992 case *American Lung Association v. Pete Wilson*, the initiative's defenders charged that Wilson's diversions were illegal. The Superior Court in Sacramento agreed and ordered the Department of Health Services to restore the media campaign. But the decision did not stop the diversions.

In 1994, the legislature passed and Governor Wilson approved AB 816, which diverted $32 million per year from Proposition 99's Health Education Account and $27 million per year from its Research Account to pay for medical care for the poor over a two-year period. The "Just Say No to Tobacco Dough Campaign," Americans for Non-Smokers' Rights, and the American Lung Association again charged that AB 816 was illegal. The latter two organizations sued the state over AB 816's diversions and won. Their case against the state was helped by testimony such as that of Dr. Lester Breslow, former director of the Department of Health Services and former dean of the UCLA School of Public Health:[6]

Once the Health Education money is received by CHDP, there is no
statutory requirement that it be used for health education. Rather, the
enabling statutes make it clear that the money is to be used to expand
(dramatically) the population eligible to receive health screening examinations....In my opinion, based on my experience both as a physician
and as an administrator, this mandate is simply a facade to evade the intent of Proposition 99.

The court barred almost all further use of Health Education Account
and Research Account funds for medical care.

At first, the Wilson Administration appealed the Superior Court's decision. Later, they attempted to defy it. In 1995, Governor Wilson sent a letter to Assembly and Senate leaders, urging that they evade the Superior
Court's decision (Just Say No To Tobacco Dough Campaign 1996). The
American Lung Association, upon learning of the action, accused the governor of trying to "subvert the Constitution" (Just Say No To Tobacco Dough
Campaign 1996).

Later the same year, the legislature passed and Governor Wilson approved SB 493, which reduced the Health Education Account's claim on
Proposition 99 money from 20 to 10 percent of revenues and reduced the
Research Account's share from 5 to 1 percent, for a total diversion of $63.7
million. Legislators argued that the diversions were justified, as the number
of poor people without health insurance shot up between 1988 and 1993,
while tobacco consumption decreased by 27 percent (Ainsworth 1996). They
did not explain why the state would want to risk erasing gains in the anti-
smoking campaign or why the money to increase the scope of health insurance should come from tobacco education programs and research, rather
than some other source. Again the American Lung Association and Americans for Non-Smokers' Rights sued the state to reverse the diversions and
again they won.

As with AB 816, the state appealed the Superior Court ruling on SB
493. The Court of Appeals for the Third District handled both appeals in
1996. It ruled that AB 816 was illegal because it did not comply with the California Constitution's procedure for amending a statutory enactment (*American Lung Association v. Pete Wilson, 1996*). The state did not appeal that
decision to the California Supreme Court, and the Court's decision that the
diversion was illegal stands today. In the case of SB 493, by contrast, the
Court of Appeals found that the state followed the proper procedure for
amending the statute. The Court, therefore, allowed the reduced tax shares
for the Health Education Account and the Research Account to stand (*Americans for Nonsmokers' Rights v. State of California, 1996*). Proposition 99's supporters appealed to the California Supreme Court, which agreed to review
the case. The state Supreme Court later vacated the order granting review
and remanded the case to the Court of Appeals for the Third District (Just
Say No to Tobacco Dough Campaign 1996). That court remitted the case to

the Sacramento County Superior Court, where it remains pending as of this writing.

To summarize, state government actors have repeatedly diverted substantial sums of tobacco surtax revenues from the programs described in Proposition 99. Although the threat of sanctions for noncompliance with the initiative is high, it appears that politicians weighed these potential sanctions against the political costs of making the tobacco industry their enemy. For many, the costs associated with compliance outweighed the sanctions that noncompliance would bring. When the courts intervened, however, the sanctions associated with noncompliance, a series of judicial rebukes of legislative actions, became more severe. The courts' intervention did not stop government actors from attempting to divert Proposition 99's funds, but did force them to change the way in which they did it, as we see from the difference between SB 493 and previous diversion attempts. If the courts ultimately rule against the state in the case of SB 493, then government actors will have an even greater incentive to comply with Proposition 99. But if history is any indication, some will seek new ways of bypassing the initiative's instructions.

NOTES

1. Most of the mandated activities simply involved funding for existing programs.
2. Data from Third Amended Complaint in *Just Say No to Tobacco Dough Campaign et al. v. State of California et al.*, Superior Court, State of California, County of Sacramento, No. 539577.
3. *Just Say No to Tobacco Dough Campaign*, Case History. All materials pertaining to this case were provided by Gwilliam, Ivary, Chiosso, Cavalli, and Brewer (counsel for the plaintiffs), of Oakland, California.
4. Opinion letter 19067, to Assemblyman Phillip Isenberg (D-Sacramento).
5. *Just Say No to Tobacco Dough Campaign*, Third Amended Complaint, pp. 25–6.
6. *Just Say No to Tobacco Dough Campaign*, History of Litigation, pp. 32–3.

8

Proposition 116 of 1990, Transportation/ Light Rail

BACKGROUND

Fed up with traffic congestion and air pollution, voters approved Proposition 116 in the 1990 primary. The initiative authorized the state to sell up to $1.99 billion in general obligation bonds to fund mass transit projects across the state. Proposition 116 specified dozens of projects that would qualify for funding and stated the maximum amount allowed for each project. In total, the measure dedicated $1.85 billion to rail projects, $73 million to nonurban county transit, $30 million to waterborne ferry projects, $20 million to a competitive bicycle program, $5 million to a state rail museum, and $10 million to CTC/Caltrans for administrative costs.

The initiative charged the California Transportation Commission (CTC) with carrying out the grant program. Agencies named in the initiative were required to submit formal applications to the CTC, and the CTC had to establish a review process for evaluating the applications. The initiative originally required the CTC to complete the approval and allocation process by July 1, 2000, a deadline that was recently extended to 2001.

Proposition 116 was one of three measures on the June 1990 ballot dealing with transportation issues. This initiative was written and sponsored by the Planning and Conservation League, a nonprofit statewide alliance of nearly 10,000 citizens and 120 conservation groups. It also received financial backing from the Southern Pacific railroad (who stood to reap significant financial benefits from Proposition 116's proposed programs). Although the three transportation measures did not directly conflict, over the course of the campaign they were presented as competing with one another. Towards the end of the campaign, Governor George Deukmejian came out in opposition to Proposition 116, as did many other legislative leaders. On Election Day, Proposition 116 won with 53.3 percent of the vote cast.

EXPECTATIONS

Although Proposition 116's electoral majority was slim, there are a number of reasons to expect a high level of compliance. First, the initiative could not have been clearer. It specified exactly what programs would qualify for funding, and in what amounts. It gave the CTC explicit instructions for soliciting and evaluating proposals, and designated a long time period for allocating the funds. Second, Proposition 116 created a number of highly interested stakeholders—the localities who were potential grantees under the initiative and the transportation companies that would provide expanded service. Each would receive substantial benefits if government actors implemented the initiative. These beneficiaries signaled their willingness and ability to mobilize resources on the issue by contributing over $2.5 million to the Proposition 116 campaign. These same interests therefore represent a credible threat of sanctions for noncompliance. Third, the technical costs of the initiative were significant but not overwhelming, as administration of the grant program would be carried out by an existing agency. And fourth, the political costs were also low. The budgetary impact of the initiative was high—$218 million annually in principal and interest on the bonds.[1] This amount, however, is only a small portion of the total cost of the program (nearly $2 billion in 1990 dollars). And what could be more attractive for term-limited politicians than a program whose benefits were immediate and whose full costs would not be felt during their time in office?

One factor, however, stood in the way of full compliance with Proposition 116. The initiative required the individual grantee agencies to submit formal applications to receive funding for the designated programs, and in some cases required the grantees to provide matching funds. Arguably, these requirements were not very onerous, given the millions (in some cases, tens of millions) of dollars the individual agencies stood to gain. Nevertheless, Prediction 4 of Chapter 3 tells us that as the number of agents responsible for implementing and enforcing an initiative increases, the probability of full compliance will decrease.

WHAT HAPPENED

The level of compliance with Proposition 116 has been high. Government actions taken in reaction to it have been consistent with the voters' mandate. Most of the organizations and counties eligible to apply for funds have done so. As of December 1999, the CTC had approved 451 individual applications totaling $1.79 billion, or 89 percent of the $1.99 billion authorized. Of the $1.79 billion approved, $50 million or approximately 3 percent had not yet been allocated. Table 8.1 shows the amounts approved and allocated to date for each of the five programs (plus administrative costs).

The amounts reported in Table 8.1 show nothing out of line with the stated intentions of Proposition 116. It does not appear from this table that state or local administrators have tried to circumvent Proposition 116; to the contrary, the CTC staff have actively solicited grant applications from the remaining qualified agencies to try to meet the initiative's funding deadline.

Indeed, a lesson to draw from Table 8.1 and the state's experience with Proposition 116 is that it can sometimes be hard to give money away. Most of the funds remaining to be approved and allocated are designated for the rail program, the largest and most diverse of the five programs. Ten years after the passage of Proposition 116, over $200 million of the voter-approved funds remain unclaimed, because some agencies failed to conform to the CTC's formal application procedures. Many of these (local and re-

Table 8.1 Implementation of Proposition 116, 1990

Program	Amount Approved by Voters (millions)	Applications Approved (millions)	Allocations Made (millions)
Rail	$1,850.0	$1,658.2	$1612.5
Nonurban	73.0	72.9	69.1
Ferry	30.0	20.0	19.8
Bicycle	20.0	30.0	29.7
Museum	5.0	0.0	0.0
Administration	10.0	8.0	8.0

gional) agencies were not as able to pay the technical costs of compliance as the proponents of Proposition 116 envisioned. Had they been able to do so, it is likely that Proposition 116 would have been fully implemented by the original deadline. However, with no sanctions or legislative opponents on the horizon, we expect full implementation of Proposition 116 in the near future.

NOTES

1. $218 million is 1998 real dollars. The 1990 nominal amount (all other figures in these cases are in nominal dollars) is $180 million.

9

Proposition 140
of 1990, Legislative
Spending Provision

BACKGROUND

In 1990, voters passed Proposition 140 in an attempt to limit what many perceived as unfair electoral advantages to incumbent state legislators. Proposition 140 was one of two term limits measures on the 1990 general election
ballot.[1] It was written by Los Angeles County Supervisor Peter Schabarum,
who contributed over $500,000 of his own money to the "Yes on 140" cam-
paign. A Washington, D.C. organization, Citizens for Congressional Reform, also provided substantial financial backing. As is true for most term
limits initiatives, almost all incumbent legislators opposed it.

Ballot arguments in favor of Proposition 140 declared that incumbent
state legislators use unfair advantages to become virtually unbeatable in
elections, thereby weakening accountability and generating a host of evils.
To reduce these perceived advantages, Proposition 140 imposed term limits
on elected state officeholders, reduced the value of legislators' retirement

benefits, and limited the amount that the state could spend on legislative salaries, staff, and expenses.

The California Supreme Court, in *Legislature of the State of California v. March Fong Eu,* found the legislative retirement benefits provision unconstitutional, but upheld the other major provisions as valid. The U.S. Supreme Court refused to hear the Legislature's appeal of the case and a subsequent case challenging the initial decision (*Bates v. Jones* 95-2638). In the next chapter, we study compliance with Proposition 140's term limits provision. In this chapter, we study government actors' response to Proposition 140's restrictions on legislative spending.

Proposition 140 limits total spending on the legislature to the lesser of 80 percent of the previous year's expenditures for these purposes or $950,000 for each member of the legislature. Given that there are 80 Assembly members and 40 Senators, the spending limit for the first year was $114 million. Proposition 140 allows this amount to increase annually by no more than the amount allowed by the State Appropriations Limit (which was the result of 1979's Proposition 4, described in Chapter 14).

Proposition 140's language makes clear that the intent of the spending cap is to reduce the advantage conferred by incumbents' access to "the 3,000 political staffers who serve the legislature in Sacramento" (California Secretary of State 1990, p. 70). But the spending limit clause specifies only that *overall* legislative spending must not exceed the mandated level (California Secretary of State 1990). The legislation does not explicitly state that spending on *political* staff must be reduced, only that total spending must be reduced. This language leaves the legislature some wiggle room regarding how they fund their activities. Given the strong bipartisan opposition to this measure, we would expect them to take full advantage.

EXPECTATIONS

Proposition 140 was one for which the threat of sanctions from organized interest groups for noncompliance was considerable. Proponents spent over $2.5 million in favor of Proposition 140. As we discussed above, a large portion of these funds came from two sources: LA County Supervisor Peter Schabarum and the Washington, D.C.-based Citizens for Congressional Reform. Through their financial support of Proposition 140, these supporters signaled that they were highly motivated and had access to substantial resources to sanction state policymakers for noncompliance.

Nevertheless, observing compliance with the legislative spending cap proved extremely difficult for several reasons.

First, as we mentioned above, the initiative was not specific about the type of staff that should be cut. Therefore, the legislature, in choosing what activities to cut, had many options. Most important, because the initiative did not specifically mandate cuts in political staff, the legislature could choose to cut nonpolitical expenses and remain within the letter (if not the spirit) of the law.

Second, tracking legislative spending and verifying implementation is difficult even for motivated and well-informed observers. Spending decisions are contained within the state's official budget. Like all government budgets, California's is extremely complex. As we will illustrate below, the basic components of the budget—line items—change over time and many are easy to manipulate. Items are constantly added, eliminated, combined, and redefined in response to the state's evolving political landscape. This fluidity of the budget makes it extremely difficult to know exactly how much the legislature is spending on a range of specific activities. At the same time, this lack of transparency in compliance allows legislators to argue that they are implementing Proposition 140's instructions, though a closer look suggests otherwise.

Another barrier to compliance is the high political and technical costs associated with the spending cap. The technical costs involve dismantling several legislative support programs or relocating their functions elsewhere in government. The political costs involve major cuts in spending on political staff. Groups that had benefited from these expenditures in the past (e.g., individual staffers, political parties, and perhaps some political constituents) would suffer. These high political and technical costs, together with the low probability of observing noncompliance, created opportunities for state policymakers to circumvent the legislative spending component of Proposition 140.

WHAT HAPPENED

Compliance with the spending cap component of Proposition 140 has indeed been partial. In the fiscal year following the initiative's passage, funding for the state legislature was cut from $166 million to the $114 million that Proposition 140 required. To soften the blow of this cut, the legislature relied on its discretion over the budget process and responded largely by slashing nonpolitical staff. The year after Proposition 140's passage, for example, funding for the nonpartisan Legislative Analyst's Office's budget was reduced by 55 percent. But many nonpolitical services of this kind were quickly recovered. For example, some of the research services formerly performed by the Legislative Analyst's Office were replaced with the creation of the California Research Bureau within the California State Library.

By reclassifying agencies and moving their budgets outside the realm of formal legislative spending, the legislature largely circumvented the intent behind Proposition 140's spending limits. In doing so, they not only managed to maintain their political staffs, they also retained the services of the agencies whose funding they cut.

Creative accounting such as this is not unusual for governments. It does, however, cause problems for people who want to use initiatives to achieve cuts in particular programs, especially when policymakers oppose the cuts. Legislatures (and, in many cases, the governor) have much discretion in how to account for and budget their activities. They have broad authority to create, combine, collapse, or erase budget line items.

A brief overview of budgeting for the Legislative Analyst's Office immediately before and after Proposition 140 illustrates the enormous difficulty inherent in trying to monitor compliance with the spending limitation. Each year, the state's budget contains Budget Item "0100 Legislature," which includes legislative spending. In the fiscal year just before imposition of Proposition 140's spending limit (fiscal year 90–91),[2] spending for the LAO is not specifically detailed. Rather, it is included within spending for the Joint Legislative Budget Committee (the committee that the LAO serves). The words "Legislative Analyst's Office" do not appear in the budget.

The following year (fiscal year 91–92), with Proposition 140's limit in place, spending on the Joint Legislative Budget Committee dropped from $7,546,000 to $1,431,000—apparently, a large reduction in spending. The new budget, however, also featured Budget Item "0157 Control Section 33.50—Auditor General and the Legislative Analyst." This budget item (0157) had not appeared in prior budgets, and the expenditures listed within it were not included in the total for Budget Item 0100. Item 0157 budgeted $7,700,000 explicitly for the Legislative Analyst's Office and the Auditor General—which more than offset the reduction in spending on the joint Legislative Budget Committee.[3]

At the same time the legislature shifted the Legislative Analyst's Office to Budget item 0157, it created the California Research Bureau (CRB) as a sub-unit of the California State Library. As mentioned above, the Bureau's function is to provide "nonpartisan analytical research...on major state issues to both houses of the Legislature..." (*Governor's Budget for 1993–94*, p. E11). But the budget does not specify the amount to be spent on the CRB; rather, it says that part of the amount budgeted for State Library Services (SLS) is to go to the CRB (the CRB is listed as a new service under the heading "State Library Services"). The amount spent on CRB is suggested by the fact that at the same time the CRB was added to SLS, the amount budgeted for SLS jumped roughly $3 million from its level in each of the previous two years. Though the budget line item for the Legislature is, on its face, in compliance with the spending limits of Proposition 140, it is clear that *at least some* of the apparent reductions were simply reallocations to different budget items.

An implicit assumption by Proposition 140's proponents was that spending reductions would cut into political staff. This didn't happen. Instead, the legislature cut nonpolitical staff spending, then partially reinstated it elsewhere in the guise of nonlegislative spending. And because the initiative was not clear about specifically what functions were to be cut, the legislature retained discretion to implement the spending cuts in a way that was more consistent with its own interests. Although the initiatives proponents may have succeeded in changing the allocation of resources for certain activities, they failed in their ultimate goal of reducing many of the benefits that a large political staff confers on incumbent state legislators.

NOTES

1. The other, Proposition 131, was placed on the ballot by the legislature as a moderate alternative to Proposition 140. Proposition 131 excluded many of Proposition 140's most punitive provisions. Voters rejected Proposition 131 in favor of the more stringent Proposition 140.
2. California's fiscal years run from July 1 to June 30. The budget figures we present here are "current fiscal year" figures, which reflect the Budget Act passed by the legislature and the governor for the current fiscal year. We draw these numbers from each year's *Governor's Budget*, but use the numbers listed for the year preceding the year listed on the *Governor's Budget*'s cover. We do so because the *Governor's Budget* for each year represents the governor's proposal to the legislature, and it may significantly differ from the budget bill that ultimately passes. So, for example, budget figures we present for fiscal year 90–91 are those listed under the heading "1990–91" in the *Governor's Budget* for fiscal year 91–92.
3. Item 0157 contains a footnote stating that LAO spending for the previous year is included in Budget Item 0100.

10

Proposition 140
of 1990, Term Limits
Provision

BACKGROUND

Proposition 140 was conceived as a way to reduce the perceived advantages of incumbent politicians. Its term limits component limited the number of terms a person could hold any particular statewide political office. In this chapter, we assess compliance with this component of Proposition 140.

The term limits component of Proposition 140 imposed the following limits:

- Members of the State Assembly can serve a maximum of three two-year terms.
- State senators and statewide officers (including governor, lieutenant governor, attorney general, controller, secretary of state, treasurer, superintendent of public instruction, and members of the Board of Equalization) can serve a maximum of two four-year terms.

- All of these limits are lifetime bans, meaning that a person who has served the maximum number of terms in an office must leave office and may never hold that office again.

EXPECTATIONS

Whereas budget actors were able to exert substantial discretion in implementing the legislative spending component of Proposition 140, such opportunities were not available with respect to the term limits provision. Policymakers in the legislative and executive branches were virtually unanimous in their opposition to the initiative. However, the expected sanctions for failing to implement and enforce the term limits component of Proposition 140 were extremely high. The probability that voters and interest groups would observe noncompliance was great, because the criteria were specific, clear, and easy to observe (either elected officials left office when they were supposed to or they did not). Public support for the measure was not overwhelming, with only 52.2 percent voting in favor of limits, but the initiative's proponents were powerful. They spent over $2.5 million to support Proposition 140 during the campaign and were part of a national term limits movement that was unlikely to back down from a challenge. More importantly, the courts raised the specter of sanctions substantially by upholding the measure in repeated court challenges. Together, these factors should have been sufficient to induce government actors to abide by Proposition 140's term limits provision, despite their solid opposition.

WHAT HAPPENED

Given the strong opposition from legislators and executive branch officials to implementing term limits, but the high political risks of simply ignoring the mandate, it is not surprising that the initial response by state policymakers was to file lawsuits seeking to overturn Proposition 140's term limits component. However, the state Supreme Court quickly upheld the limits (*Legislature of the State of California v. March Fong Eu*, 1991). After the U.S. Supreme Court struck down term limits imposed by states on their own members of Congress, California legislators again challenged the Proposition 140 limits—this time in federal court. Despite initially favorable rulings, however, the Court of Appeals for the Ninth Circuit, hearing the case *en banc*, upheld Proposition 140's limits.[1] The U.S. Supreme Court's subsequent refusal to hear an appeal of the decision means that the Proposition 140 limits remain (*Bates v. Jones* 1997). In fact, the limits were already in effect and had already led to a complete turnover in the legislature by the time the Court of Appeals issued its ruling in 1997. Thus, although most legislators were strongly opposed to term limits, the threat of severe sanctions forced them to comply.

NOTES

1. In the Ninth Circuit, an *en banc* hearing consists of a panel of eleven judges, rather than the usual three. *En banc* hearings tend to be reserved for important or controversial cases, or for cases in which the three judge panel is divided.

11

Proposition 184 of 1994, Three Strikes

BACKGROUND

In the wake of rising crime rates and the much-publicized murder of a young girl, Polly Klaas, by a convicted criminal who had been released from jail, voters in November 1994 overwhelmingly approved Proposition 184, also known as the "Three Strikes" initiative. The Proposition's goals were to ensure that repeat criminal offenders are sentenced to lengthy jail terms and to limit the ability of judges to reduce or eliminate the punishments imposed on such criminals. A broad coalition of law enforcement officers, victim's organizations, and taxpayer groups supported the initiative. Its chief spokesman, Mike Reynolds, was the father of an 18-year-old murder victim.

Once Proposition 184's proponents began their campaign, it became clear that bipartisan public support for Three Strikes legislation was overwhelming. Not wanting to miss this important political opportunity, the legislature passed and the governor signed in March 1994 a bill containing virtually identical legislation. Therefore, by the time it was voted on, Proposition 184 simply reaffirmed existing legislation. Indeed, the only difference between the legislators' bill and the initiative is that initiatives are more difficult to amend than regular legislation—they require a subsequent vote of the people. This is why Proposition 184's proponents continued to campaign for their initiative after the legislature acted; Proposition 184's passage ensured that the Three Strikes legislation could not be altered by future legislatures.

The initiative is brief and to the point. It specifies that:

1. If a person is convicted of a serious or violent felony (a "strike") and has previous strikes, the sentence for the current conviction must be imposed *consecutive to*, rather than *concurrent with*, any pending prison sentences.[1]
2. If a person is convicted of a second strike, the sentence for the current conviction will be double the length that would normally be imposed for that conviction.
3. If a person is convicted of a third (or greater) strike,[2] he or she is subject to a minimum sentence of 25 years-to-life, and under many circumstances is subject to a much longer sentence.
4. Certain specified crimes committed as a minor are to be counted as strikes.
5. Persons convicted of multiple strikes cannot be granted probation, committed to any facility other than state prison (e.g., mental institutions or rehabilitation programs), or have their sentences reduced because of the length of time between convictions.
6. Prosecuting attorneys "shall plead and prove each prior felony conviction," but "may move to dismiss or strike a prior felony conviction allegation in the furtherance of justice pursuant to Section 1385 [of the California Penal Code], or if there is insufficient evidence to prove the prior conviction." If the court is satisfied that the evidence is insufficient, it may dismiss the prior strike for sentencing purposes.

EXPECTATIONS

The potential sanctions for not complying with the voters' directive are quite high for both the governor and the legislature. An overwhelming 71.9 percent of voters supported the measure, and this support cut across partisan and geographic lines. A Field Poll conducted shortly before the election showed that 74 percent of Democrats and 83 percent of Republicans (79 percent of Californians overall) reported being "extremely concerned" with "crime and law enforcement," making it the issue of greatest concern to Californians at that time (Field Institute, August 1994). At least 60 percent of voters voted for the proposition in all but five of the state's 58 counties. The five counties with the lowest approval rates were San Francisco (42.7), Marin (52.8), Alameda (55.4), Santa Cruz (56), and Sonoma (59.4); note that only in San Francisco County did Proposition 184 get less than 50 percent of the vote.

Not only was public support intense enough to make the threat of electoral sanctions real, but the likelihood of observing compliance was also high. The language of the Three Strikes law is clear and concise, as noted by California Supreme Court Chief Justice Ronald M. George in an opinion for the Court. "The courts of this state on occasion have found fault with the imprecise nature of language contained within statutory enactments," George wrote. "We find it difficult, however, to imagine language clearer, or more unequivocal, than that [of the Three Strikes law]" (*People v. Benson* 1998). Combined with the high salience and public concern regarding the issue, this makes it likely that interested parties such as the initiative's supporters, the media, victims' rights groups, or ambitious prosecutors or politicians would not hesitate to seek sanctions if the legislature and governor failed to comply with Proposition 184.

However, one clause in Proposition 184 makes it difficult for proponents to establish noncompliance. As noted above, the initiative allows prosecutors and judges discretion not to count prior strikes, "in the interest of justice," when imposing sentences for current convictions. This clause creates wiggle room for prosecutors and judges who do not favor full compliance.

The compliance costs associated with Proposition 184 are virtually zero. When the initiative passed, it simply reaffirmed a law that was already in place. In other words, the state had already agreed to pay the costs associated with the Three Strikes legislation before a single voter went to the polls, so the passage of Proposition 184 itself was not the direct cause of whatever costs Three Strikes implementation implied.

Because we want to explain the extent of compliance with the Three Strikes initiative, however, it is worthwhile to note that the costs associated with the legislation were potentially enormous. According to the Legislative Analyst, implementation and enforcement of Three Strikes legislation—either the legislature's or the initiative's version—would cost the state $200 million in the first year, growing by several hundred million each year for 32 years. By 2026, additional costs could reach $6 billion per year. In addition, the state would need to incur one-time costs of about $20 billion for new prison construction.

The political costs of compliance with Three Strikes legislation are more complex. As we discussed above, full compliance stands to cost taxpayers hundreds of millions of dollars. As with all spending programs, the legislature and governor must make budgetary trade-offs, taking resources from existing programs to pay for this new program or raising new revenues from additional taxes. In most cases, either course of action creates enemies and raises political tensions.

In the case of Proposition 184, few powerful constituents opposed increased spending on prisons. Indeed, support for Three Strikes cut across many constituencies. At the time that Proposition 184 was passed, many Democrats joined Republicans in taking a hard line on crime and punishment, generating bipartisan support for tougher anti-crime measures. As a result, this aspect of the political costs of complying with Three Strikes was relatively low.

Most of the important compliance decisions made with respect to Proposition 184 are, however, made by neither the legislature nor the governor. They are made by individuals—district attorneys and judges—who argue for and impose criminal sentences. Many district attorneys and judges come from areas with strong voter support for Three Strikes and thus have compelling electoral reasons to enforce the law. However, not *all* district attorneys and judges have such strong incentives. In areas where support for the law is low, such as San Francisco, electoral pressures may create incentives for district attorneys and judges to block enforcement.[3] In addition, to the extent that juries in such areas reflect the voters' preferences, we might expect it to be harder to obtain "third strike" convictions in areas where more people opposed Proposition 184. We therefore expect compliance with Three Strikes to be mixed, with greater compliance in places where more voters supported the initiative.

WHAT HAPPENED

To assess compliance with Three Strikes, we must think carefully about what compliance means in this context. The law states that *if a person is convicted of a strike and is found to have at least one prior strike, then that person will receive a long sentence.* For analytic purposes, it is useful to break these conditions down into three components: being convicted, being found to have at least one prior strike, and being given a long sentence. We examine them in reverse order.

Long Sentences

Much of the attention given to enforcement of Three Strikes focuses on the lengths of sentences given to those convicted of a third felony. For instance, one study, seeking to examine the effects of local levels of compliance on local crime rates, operationalizes enforcement as the number of cases per county in which Three Strikes sentencing rules were applied (Justice Policy Institute 1999). Also, a great deal of media attention has focused on cases in which life sentences were handed out to criminals who committed relatively minor crimes that nonetheless qualified as third strikes. In one much-publicized case, for instance, defendant Russell Benson was sentenced to 25-years-to-life for shoplifting a $20 carton of cigarettes (he had been convicted of two felony counts resulting from a burglary and stabbing in 1979); in 1998 the State Supreme Court upheld his conviction (*People v. Benson* 1998).

The Courts of Appeal and the State Supreme Court have issued a series of decisions that strictly hold to the criteria that if a person is convicted of a strike and is found to have at least one prior strike, then that person will receive a long sentence.[4] These courts ruled that a trial judge has no discretion to sentence a convicted third-strike offender to probation or to a rehabilitation program "in the furtherance of justice." Rather, the trial judge must either impose the enhanced sentence mandated by Three Strikes, or find that (at least) one of the prior strikes should be dismissed for sentencing purposes (*People v. Superior Court (Roam)* 1999).

The Justice Policy Institute's statistics and the court's doctrine suggest that when felons are convicted and found to have prior strikes, long prison sentences are indeed imposed. By this criterion, there appears to be a high degree of compliance with this portion of the initiative's mandate. But this perspective misses the effects that decisions at early stages of the conviction process might have on enforcement. Specifically, since compliance requires that long sentences be meted out, *subject to a person being convicted of a strike and found to have at least one prior strike*, it is possible that district attorneys or judges wishing not to comply with Three Strikes might prevent those conditions from being met.

In what follows, we examine conviction patterns at the state and county levels. We show that while there is some evidence of compliance at the state level, these aggregate statistics mask substantial county level variation. While district attorneys and judges complied fully with Proposition 184 in some counties, their counterparts in other counties were able to exert substantial discretion and dilute the effect of the initiative. These patterns of compliance correspond closely with variations in county-level voter support for Proposition 184.

State-Level Compliance

We now consider the disposition of felony arrests during the period 1987–1996.[5] All figures presented in the following graphs are derived from the set of all felony arrests for the given geographic area and year. We begin by analyzing felony arrests in order to shed light on the stages of the conviction process at which we expect to find district attorneys differing in their decisions relative to Three Strikes.

To study compliance with Proposition 184, we would ideally analyze the arrests, charges, and dispositions of people with previous strikes. Because these data are not available, however, we proceed by assuming that the arrest rates of people with previous strikes do not vary systematically across the time period presented. In other words, we assume that police arrest patterns do not change such that repeat offenders are arrested either more or less frequently after passage of Proposition 184. Given this assumption, we interpret any changes in the charges and dispositions of those people arrested to reflect discretion being exercised by district attorneys and judges.

Figure 11.1 shows statewide trends for four types of felony arrest dispositions that bear upon implementation of Proposition 184. The trendlines report:

1. The proportion of felony arrests in which the arrestee is charged with a crime. This is one measure of the discretion being exercised by district attorneys, since they can choose not to file charges if they expect those charges to bring a Three Strikes sentence that they believe is too severe.
2. The proportion of felony arrests in which the arrestee is charged with a felony. As with the previous measure, this is a way of observing dis-

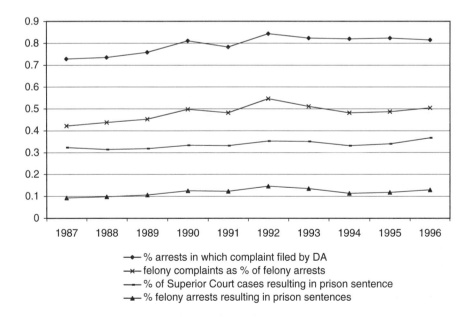

— % arrests in which complaint filed by DA
— felony complaints as % of felony arrests
— % of Superior Court cases resulting in prison sentence
— % felony arrests resulting in prison sentences

Figure 11.1   Statewide Felony Arrest Disposition

trict attorneys discretion, since they can choose to charge a felony arrestee with a lesser crime in order to avoid a Three Strikes case.

3. The proportion of Superior Court cases (again, resulting from felony arrests) that result in prison sentences. Given the available data, we cannot disaggregate misdemeanor convictions from felony convictions. Therefore, we make the additional assumption that the ratio of prison sentences for misdemeanors to prison sentences for felonies is constant over time. This assumption allows us to interpret the proportion of cases resulting in prison sentences as a measure of the proportion of Third Strike defendants who are sentenced to prison terms. Therefore, observing a drop in felonies relative to misdemeanors after Three Strikes would suggest that at least some district attorneys and judges were attempting to dilute the impact of the legislation by classifying as misdemeanors crimes that used to be classified as felonies.

4. The proportion of felony arrests that result in Superior Court prison sentences. This is the most comprehensive measure of compliance, as it begins with arrests and ends with prison sentences. Given the assumptions of the previous sections, this is an overall measure of the proportion of Three Strikes arrestees who are ultimately sentenced under Three Strikes guidelines.

As Figure 11.1 shows, the first two trends (complaints filed/felony arrests and felony complaints filed/felony arrests) are flat across the years before and after Proposition 184. The final two measures (prison sentences/Superior Court cases and prison sentences/felony arrests) increase slightly after 1994. This evidence suggests that, on average, Proposition 184 was implemented to the extent that people arrested and tried were more likely to be sentenced to prison. At a minimum, the lack of a post-1994 downturn in any of the measures suggests that, aggregated to the state level, district attorneys and judges did not systematically exercise discretion in ways that decreased compliance with Three Strikes. Given our previous arguments that the costs of implementation and enforcement should vary within the state, however, we expect these statewide figures to mask important local differences. We now examine county-level data to test this hypothesis.

County-Level Compliance

Despite its strict interpretation of the Three Strikes sentencing provision, the State Supreme Court has granted judges substantial discretion in deciding how to count prior strikes. The Court has ruled that trial judges:

- may dismiss (i.e., not count) prior strikes for sentencing purposes if such action serves "the furtherance of justice" (*People v. Superior Court (Romero)* 1996),

- may count multiple felony convictions resulting from a single incident (e.g., a violent robbery that results in convictions on both burglary and assault charges) as either one or more strikes (*People v. Benson* 1998) and
- in cases involving multiple convictions for a single crime, may impose sentences consecutively (*People v. Deloza* 1998).

The key word in each of these clauses is *may*—the Court has given trial judges significant discretion to decide such matters. These decisions are not trivial; they allow judges to hand out a considerable range of sentences for any particular crime. For example, in the *Deloza* case, the trial court's discretion to impose either concurrent or consecutive sentences amounted to discretion between imposing a 25-year-to-life sentence or a 111-year sentence (*People v. Deloza* 1998). Similarly, the ability to dismiss prior strikes when sentencing can allow judges to circumvent Three Strikes sentencing requirements altogether, meaning that options such as parole and rehabilitation programs once more become sentencing alternatives.

In the following figures, we look at the same measures of compliance presented in the previous section; but we now disaggregate the data and show trends for six different counties. We include the three counties with the lowest (San Francisco, Marin, and Alameda), and highest (Madera, 84 percent; Riverside, 82.7 percent; and Tulare, 82.2 percent) voter support for Proposition 184 in the 1994 election. For each measure, we expect to see lower levels of compliance for the three low-support counties and higher levels of compliance for the high-support counties.

Figure 11.2 shows the proportion of felony arrests in which complaints were filed. As expected, fewer complaints were filed in the low-support counties. In every year, the proportion for San Francisco (whose district attorney, Terence Hallinan, was one of the only district attorneys in the state to oppose Three Strikes publicly) is lower than for any of the other counties. Similarly, Alameda is always lower than any county other than San Francisco; Marin is always lower than two of the three high-support counties; and, Marin is lower than all three high-support counties in the post-preposition 184 period.

Figure 11.3 shows the proportion of felony arrests that resulted in a felony complaint being filed. Again, as we expect, the proportion of felony charges filed is almost always lower in the low-support than in the high-support counties. San Francisco and Alameda always fall below all the high-support counties; Marin always falls below two of the three high-support counties; and Marin is below all three high-support counties in the post-184 period.

Figure 11.4 shows the proportion of Superior Court cases that resulted in prison sentences. We expect the low-support counties to impose fewer

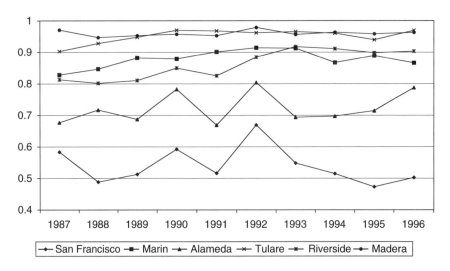

Figure 11.2   Percent of Felony Arrests in which a Complaint Was Filed by D.A.

prison sentences. With the exception of two years (each of which saw one low-support county slightly above one high-support county), the low-support counties always fall below the high-support counties.

Figure 11.5 shows the proportion of felony arrests leading to Superior Court prison sentences. As we discussed above, this is our most comprehen-

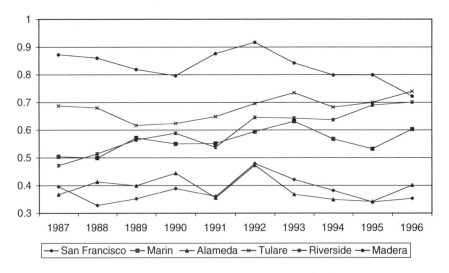

Figure 11.3   Felony Complaints as Percentage of Felony Arrests

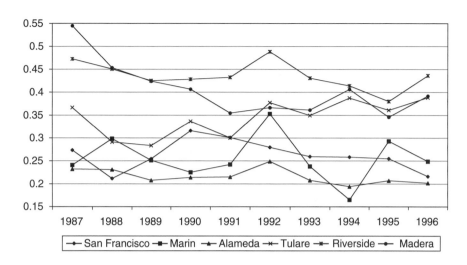

Figure 11.4 Percent of Superior Court Cases Resulting in Prison Sentence

sive measure of compliance as it captures the discretion of both district attorneys and judges throughout the process leading from arrest to Three Strikes sentencing. In this case, lower levels of compliance mean proportionally fewer prison sentences. Here, the pattern that we see in the previous figures is even more stark. All three low-support counties fall below all

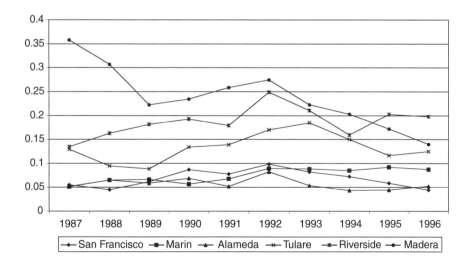

Figure 11.5 Percent of Felony Arrests Resulting in Superior Court Prison Sentence

three high-support counties in every year; moreover, the rate of prison sentences in high-support counties is typically two to three times the rate in low-support counties.

To summarize, state policymakers complied with Proposition 184 to the extent that they were empowered to do so. District attorneys and judges at the local level, however, also make important decisions about compliance. Language in the proposition and decisions by the State Supreme Court grant these actors substantial discretion in how to treat prior strikes. And, indeed, we find mixed compliance with the initiative in the sense that the actions of local officials have led to different levels of compliance across various geographic areas of the state. We observe greater compliance with Proposition 184 in counties where voter support was high and less compliance where voter support was low.

NOTES

1. The statute specifies that "serious or violent felonies" refers to a specific list of crimes, and definition of these terms is given in the California Penal Code. Therefore, this terminology is not as ambiguous as it may at first appear.
2. Strikes refer to those convictions occurring before, as well as after, the passage of Proposition 184; therefore, many people had far more than three strikes when the measure passed. The law does not retroactively affect sentences for those with multiple strikes at the time of passage.
3. Superior Court judges are elected to six-year terms in competitive elections (meaning that another candidate can run against them). When there is a mid-term vacancy, however, the Governor appoints a judge to finish the term (Syer and Culver 1992, 267).
4. See *People v. Hazelton* 1996, *Garcia v. Superior Court of Orange County* 1997, *People v. Fuhrman* 1997.
5. Data for the years 1987 through 1992 are taken from California Bureau of Criminal Statistics 1993. Data for subsequent years were provided by the Criminal Justice Statistics Center of the state Department of Justice.

12

Proposition 198 of 1996, Open Primaries

BACKGROUND

In 1996, voters passed Proposition 198, the Open Primary Act. Proposition 198 requires nominations for federal, statewide, and state legislative offices to be open to all registered voters. It requires the state to use a "blanket" ballot, listing all candidates for a given office together on a single ballot. All registered voters, regardless of their partisan registration, receive the same ballot and can cast their vote for any candidate of any party.[1] The top vote-getter from each party for each office receives the party's nomination for that office and advances to the general election. A similar system is used in Alaska and Washington.

Proposition 198 passed with little fanfare. Its proponents spent about $1 million, while opponents spent only $50,000 (California Secretary of State 1996a). The measure received 59.5 percent of the vote (California Secretary of State 1996b).

More interesting than the character of the campaign (or lack thereof) were the people involved. Proponents included numerous individuals known for their lack of party affiliations.[2] They argued that the open or "blanket" primary would reduce political control by party elites; allow participation by independent and minor party voters; and result in more moderate elected representatives. Opponents included the "who's who" of the state's partisan establishment.[3] Virtually all of the state's political parties—major and minor, left and right—opposed the blanket primary. They argued that the blanket primary would open the nomination process to partisan mischief and undermine the parties' abilities to choose their own standard bearers.

After the initiative passed, it was challenged in federal court by the California Democratic Party, the California Republican Party, the Libertarian Party, and the Peace and Freedom Party. The arguments presented in the case were both constitutional (i.e., that the law violates the parties' implied First Amendment rights of association) and political (i.e., that it would create mischief in the electoral process). The initiative was upheld in District Court and the Ninth Circuit, and a request for a hearing *en banc* was denied. At the time of this writing, the U.S. Supreme Court had just completed its collection of testimony in the case.

EXPECTATIONS

The technical and political costs of implementing and enforcing Proposition 198 were moderate. The technical costs involved matters such as reprinting the ballots and redesigning the process for counting ballots. The initiative did not require the creation of any new agencies, programs, or regulatory structures. Political costs were also low, as the measure involved little budgetary impact. Still, even though the costs of complying with the mandate were low, elected officials and candidates for office opposed Proposition 198 nearly unanimously. A few renegade politicians came out in support of the initiative; but none of the outspoken supporters were incumbent members of the legislature or the executive branch. Therefore, it seems safe to assume that both the legislature and the governor opposed Proposition 198 when it came time to decide whether to comply with the initiative.

Given that both the legislature and the governor opposed Proposition 198, the question of compliance turns on the expectation of sanctions. Was the proponents' threat of sanctions sufficiently high to compel state policymakers to implement and enforce an initiative they opposed? Recall that when state policymakers assess the expected sanctions for noncompliance, two considerations are relevant.

First, they consider whether compliance is easy to observe. Proposition 198 allows little room for interpretation. It dictates that "all persons entitled to vote, including those not affiliated with any political party, shall have the right to vote at any election for any candidate regardless of the candidate's political affiliation." It also "provides for a single primary ballot on which, under the appropriate title for each office, the names and party affiliations of all candidates are placed randomly and not grouped by political party" (California Secretary of State 1996b). The fact that every voter can observe whether the ballots are in compliance reinforces the idea that noncompliance would be easy to observe.

Second, government actors must consider whether proponents can amass resources sufficient to punish them if noncompliance is observed. Proponents of Proposition 198 were not, for the most part, well-funded special interest groups with large budgets and deep pockets. Proponents raised less than a million dollars over the course of the campaign. Granted, they might have raised and spent more money if passage of the measure began to look uncertain. Still, the fact that they didn't raise more money at least meant that their ability to do so was not obvious. Further, the level and intensity of voter support was also uncertain. Proposition 198 passed by a comfortable margin, receiving nearly 60 percent of the vote. But, given the low intensity and minimal grassroots mobilization undertaken during the campaign, it is far from clear that voters would be willing to take costly action to punish state policymakers for noncompliance. The one resource that Proposition 198's proponents did have was the threat of legal sanctions. As we show below, the courts have consistently ruled in favor of the proponents, arming them with the threat of legal sanctions for noncompliance.

WHAT HAPPENED

At a number of stages, the legislature tried not to comply with Proposition 198's mandate. The legislative parties and leadership challenged the law immediately and vigorously. The executive branch did, however, provide substantial resources (via then-Attorney General Dan Lungren) to defend the law. Lungren defended Proposition 198 despite the fact that he personally opposed the initiative. The moment that Proposition 198 passed, however, it became the official law of the state and, hence, it was the Attorney General's responsibility to defend. After he prevailed in federal court, the state enforced the law, holding its first blanket primary in 1998.

In the meantime, outside actors—the national political parties—increased the costs of compliance with Proposition 198. The national parties threatened not to seat California's delegation to their presidential nominating conventions if delegates were selected in a blanket primary. So, even after the courts upheld the law and forced the legislature and the executive into compliance, the state legislature continued to resist Proposition 198's mandate.

The legislature passed subsequent legislation (SB 1505 of 1998) to exempt the presidential primary from Proposition 198's blanket primary requirement. Since the law amended Proposition 198's instructions, however, the presidential primary exemption required voter approval. In November

1998, voters solidly defeated the referendum, Proposition 3, which amassed only 46.1 percent of the vote.

Afterwards, Secretary of State Bill Jones suggested an alternative to the closed presidential primary—identify the voter's party registration on the blanket ballots and separately count the major party members' ballots for the presidential primary race. In other words, Proposition 198's ballots will not be disturbed; but the major parties could be selective about how they count the votes recorded on those ballots. This procedure for counting ballots was used in California's 2000 presidential primary and has not yet been tested in the courts.

To summarize, the legislature took numerous steps to avoid complying with Proposition 198. In the end, state officeholders were forced to comply under the threat of legal sanctions. Had the Court not intervened, it would have been interesting to see whether the state would have found other ways to reinterpret or ignore the measure.

The national parties were also forced to comply, in that they could not compel the state to overturn the initiative. In the end, however, the initiative had no force over the manner in which the parties used the new ballots. The national parties are counting the ballots in a way that Proposition 198's proponents may not have anticipated. So, for the 2000 presidential primaries at least, the intent of Proposition 198's proponents is less than fully realized. [As this volume went to press, the U.S. Supreme Court overturned Proposition 198. While their decision does not nullify the 1998 and 2000 election results, it does imply that only registered party members can participate in future California primaries.]

NOTES

1. In fact, the two major parties still have separate ballots. Political party central and district committee members are still nominated in closed primaries. The partisan ballots differ from the blanket ballots only on these races for party officials.
2. The ballot arguments in favor of the measure were signed by Becky Morgan, former state senator; Eugene Lee, Emeritus Professor; Dan Stanford, former chairman of the California Fair Political Practices Commission; Lucy Killea, former state senator; and Houston Flournoy, former state controller.
3. Ballot arguments against the initiative were signed by Bruce Herschensohn, senior fellow at the Claremont Institute; John Van de Kamp, former California attorney general; Alison Dundes Renteln, acting director of the USC Unruh Institute of Politics; John S. Herrington, chairman, California Republican Party; and Bill Press, chair, California Democratic Party.

13

Proposition 227
of 1998, Bilingual
Education

BACKGROUND

Proposition 227 is the third "English Only" initiative passed by California voters since 1978.[1] Proposition 227 was sponsored by political maverick Ron Unz, who contributed more than $750,000 of his own money to the "Yes on 227" campaign. The measure's opponents, funded largely by the California Teachers' Association and the owner of the Spanish language television network, Univision, spent more than $5 million to oppose the initiative. On Election Day, voters approved Proposition 227 with 60.9 percent of the vote.

Proposition 227 contained two major provisions. The first eliminated the state's system of bilingual education in the public schools and replaced it with a program of "English immersion." Proponents argued that the state's current system of bilingual education, in which teachers rely heavily on students' native language in the classroom, had failed to teach English to a generation of children. As a solution, they advocated English immersion—a policy change that required teachers to use English textbooks and spoken English for instruction. The second provision established a $50 million-per-year, ten-year community-based English tutoring (CBET) program. The tutoring program was conceived as a way to help nonnative parents improve their English skills sufficiently to enable them to assist their children with their schoolwork. In this case study, we examine compliance with the first provision, Proposition 227's bilingual education component.

EXPECTATIONS

There are several reasons to expect only partial compliance with Proposition 227. First, the initiative provided vague directions to those charged with implementation. The initiative stated that school instruction was to be primarily in English, unless the child clearly did not understand the instruction. Exactly how much non-English instruction would then be allowed was unclear. The initiative also stated that parents could petition to have their children exempted from the English immersion program. It did not, however, completely specify the procedures for processing and evaluating such requests.

Second, Proposition 227 required actions from a large number of school officials. These officials were granted substantial discretion by the initiative itself. Specifically, they are able to determine the mix of English and native language to be used in different types of English immersion programs. They are also allowed to decide how to publicize and promote parents' rights to request waivers for their children.

Third, although Proposition 227 gave parents and guardians standing to sue teachers and administrators for noncompliance with the measure, monitoring to ensure compliance with specific requirements (e.g., checking to see whether a teacher is using less than or equal to 40 percent English in the classroom) could be extremely difficult. Therefore, we expect school administrators to be able to exert substantial discretion in their interpretations of Proposition 227 and, hence, school administrators who opposed the initiative to comply with it less fully than administrators who supported it.

WHAT HAPPENED

Across the state, school districts have varied in the extent to which they have implemented English immersion programs. Some districts have complied fully with Proposition 227's English immersion mandate; others have complied partially; still others have virtually ignored the mandate. At one extreme is San Francisco, where Proposition 227 received only 38.3 percent voter support. Its school superintendent, Bill Rojas, boldly stated that Proposition 227 would not be implemented, regardless of court action on it

(*San Francisco Examiner* 1998). He cited a 1970s court order commonly known as the "Lau" decision, which guaranteed to every student lessons in a language they could understand (Booth 1998). The San Francisco School Board joined Rojas, vowing to exhaust all legal channels to fight 227. "Our decision reflects the will of the people of San Francisco who voted over-whelmingly against Proposition 227," proclaimed School Board President Carlota del Portillo (San Francisco Unified School District 1998). San Francisco was joined in defiance by three Bay Area districts—Oakland, Berkeley, and Hayward—which successfully challenged Proposition 227 in Alameda County Superior Court, and by San Jose, which won a district-wide exemption to the initiative.

At the other end of the spectrum was Oceanside Unified School District (OUSD), which has implemented 227 zealously. According to an Oceanside principal who testified before Congress in June 1999, OUSD

> ...interpreted the legislation more strictly than most districts. In Oceanside, 'Structured English Immersion' classes replaced bilingual ones and all instructional materials were presented in English. Teachers were permitted to use a child's native language only when it was clear that a student did not grasp a key concept. Many California school districts utilized a "blanket" waiver approach, sending waiver forms to all English Language Learners [ELLs] and approving all waivers submitted. In Oceanside, parents were required to meet with the principal before obtaining a waiver application. Furthermore, a team of educators evaluated each student's waiver application individually. The principal, the classroom teacher, a certified bilingual instructor, and two members of our curriculum and instruction division used student assessment data, work samples, behavior, and attendance to determine if a child had a legitimate educational need for a bilingual program. This year, only five of the 155 waivers submitted were approved. The five waivers approved did not constitute enough students to form a bilingual classroom according to the new provisions of the law. Therefore, no bilingual classes were offered this year (Federal News Service 1998).

In addition to differences between school districts, there has also been great variety in implementation and enforcement within districts. Consider San Diego City Schools (SDCS 1998). As of November 24, 1998, 21 percent of the district's 37,250 English Language Learners had submitted waivers and 95 percent of those waivers had been approved. These aggregate statistics mask important variation at the level of individual schools. Of San Diego City's 163 schools, 96 held no meetings to inform parents of their rights under Proposition 227, 38 held one meeting, 19 held two, eight held three, one held five, and one held six.[2] Twenty-seven schools sent mailings to supplement district-wide mailings, and 72 used other means to inform parents and guardians. Nineteen schools approved all of the waivers they received, most of which exempted large numbers of students from the bilingual education provision of Proposition 227. Seven schools, by contrast, approved no waivers at all.[3]

There has also been great variance in the types of English immersion used in different schools and districts. In Ventura County's Hueneme school district, students granted waivers attend "hybrid" classes with a 50/50 English/Spanish split (Gorman 1999). Orange County's Robert A. Gates Elementary received a blanket exemption from Proposition 227 so that it could continue its "dual-immersion" program. At Gates, students in kindergarten and first grade have a 90/10 Spanish/English split, with the proportion in English increasing by 10 percent annually (Gorman 1999).

To summarize, in districts where parents and implementation agents prefer the English immersion program to traditional bilingual education, compliance with the initiative has been substantial. In districts where they prefer bilingual education, the vague aspects of Proposition 227 have allowed them to defy the measure's intent with no significant threat of sanctions.

NOTES

1. The others include Proposition 38 of 1984 and Proposition 63 of 1986, both of which declared English to be the state's official language. See Chapter 5 for a discussion of Proposition 63.
2. These statistics leave out charter schools, which are exempt from Proposition 227, and Metro/Choice, an untraditional school.
3. Participants at a recent conference sponsored by the University of California's Linguistic Minority Research Institute and the California Policy Research Center agreed that school districts "supportive of bilingual education before Proposition 227 have found ways in the new law to keep at least some bilingual classrooms; districts without such support, or those critical of bilingual education, have found ways in the law to get rid of it or severely restrict it." (Schnaiberg 1999).

14

Proposition 4 of 1979, Gann Limit

BACKGROUND

In response to skyrocketing property taxes and huge government budget surpluses, angry California voters in the late 1970s passed two initiatives—Proposition 13 of 1978 and Proposition 4 of 1979—aimed at reducing and limiting the size of government. In this case, we study Proposition 4, the 1979 initiative that imposed the State Appropriations Limit (SAL), which is also called the *Gann limit* after the proposition's author and chief proponent, Paul Gann. In the next chapter, we examine aspects of Proposition 13.

In contrast to Proposition 13, which limited property tax rates, Proposition 4 imposed limits on government spending and mandated that unspent revenues be returned to taxpayers. This is a particularly interesting case for our study because, unlike most of the other cases we examine, it features changes over time in the expected sanctions for noncompliance and in the political costs of implementation and enforcement. We show that compliance with the initiative tracked changes in these factors.

Proposition 4 amended the State Constitution to include the following provisions:

1. Appropriations financed by the "proceeds of taxes" may not increase, except for annual adjustments based on cost of living and population growth. This limit applies to both state and local government. Appropriation levels from fiscal year 1978–79 served as the baseline for the first year the SAL was in effect (fiscal year 1980–81).
2. Governments must return to taxpayers any revenues in excess of the SAL.
3. The state must reimburse local governments for the cost of complying with "state mandates."
4. Some types of spending are not subject to the limit. The most notable exceptions are debt payments (including voter-approved bonded debt incurred after 1979); user fees based on "reasonable costs" (California Secretary of State 1979, p. 16); benefit payments from retirement, unemployment insurance, and disability insurance funds; and spending from bond funds and special districts that do not receive any funding from the "proceeds of taxes" or that meet other specific criteria (California Secretary of State 1979, p. 20).

In this case study, we focus primarily on compliance with the first provision of Proposition 4, the State Appropriations Limit. We also briefly discuss compliance with the second provision, taxpayer refunds.

EXPECTATIONS

As noted, this case differs from others in our study inasmuch as two of the key factors in our model—sanctions for noncompliance with the SAL and the political costs of implementation and enforcement—vary over time. This leads us to expect variation in compliance over time as well.

The sanctions that government actors could expect for noncompliance with the SAL were high at the time of Proposition 4's passage. Seventy-four percent of voters approved Proposition 4 in the 1979 special election. Many voters felt that, given the huge state government budget surplus of the time, tax levels were unduly burdensome. Since the government had shown no inclination to reduce the surplus, voters sought to do so via the initiative process.

Ten years later, taxes and surpluses were no longer as important to most voters. In a 1989 Field Poll, more voters expressed concern about crime and law enforcement, public schools, and road repair than about taxes (Field Institute 1989). The Field Poll also asked:

> Suppose that the state collected more money in taxes than it is permitted to spend under the Gann limit. Would you favor giving back the extra money to taxpayers in the form of a tax rebate or would you favor al-

lowing the state to spend the extra money in areas which it feels need it the most?

Slightly more respondents favored spending on state programs (47.7 to 46.9 percent). From data such as this, we infer that the expected sanction from voters for not enforcing the SAL was markedly lower by 1989 than it was in 1979.

While public support for spending limits changed over the period that we study, the ease of observing compliance, and hence the probability of a sanction being applied, remained low throughout. There are several reasons that compliance with Proposition 4 is difficult to observe.

First, the measure is complex; it deals with many different types of revenues and spending and, more importantly, applies different rules to different spending types. It therefore requires a fairly high degree of specialization and attention just to understand what Proposition 4 is intended to do.

Second, the measure makes critical but ambiguous distinctions between "proceeds from taxes" and user/license fees. Since the initiative does not specify how this distinction is to be made, discretion over interpretation passes to the legislature and the governor.

Third, since the SAL applies differently to various types of spending, policymakers can move functions between affected and exempted programs. Proposition 4 specifies that programs moved from one spending source to another are to be subject to their original limit. However, distinguishing whether a new program is really "new" or whether it is just an old program in a new guise can be difficult (see Chapter 9 for examples of how legislatures can rename expenditures). Such flexibility further complicates the task of monitoring compliance.

Conventional wisdom holds that the SAL imposed no real constraint on government spending in its early years, because the high rates of inflation at that time kept the limit far above the state's actual spending levels. As shown in Figure 14.1, however, spending caught up with SAL spending by the mid-1980s. As this happened, compliance costs grew—the limit threatened to force the legislature and governor to make difficult budgetary decisions.

In the period before the limit caught up with spending, we expect to see high levels of compliance with the measure, since the likelihood of sanctions was high and costs were low. In contrast, once compliance became costly and public concern with government spending (and hence the likelihood of sanctions) dropped, we expect reduced compliance.

Circumstances regarding compliance with Proposition 4 changed again in 1990. In that year, the legislature placed Proposition 111 on the ballot and voters approved it. Proposition 111 increased the SAL, allowing the

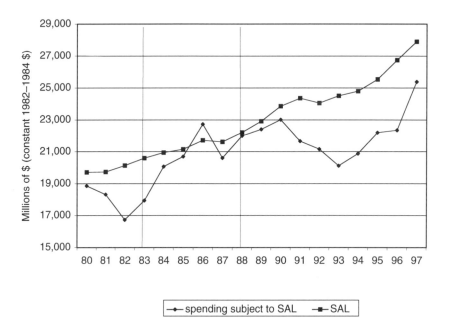

Figure 14.1   Spending Subject to SAL

government to spend more money. In effect, Proposition 111 reduced the political costs of compliance with the SAL. Given this drop in the compliance costs, we expect once again to see high levels of compliance after 1990.

WHAT HAPPENED

We now look at several measures of compliance with the SAL, and assess how compliance varies across the three periods mentioned above. Figure 14.2 compares the proportions of state spending that are and are not subject to the cap. Figure 14.2 shows two trendlines—the amount of SAL spending and the amount of overall state spending. The dashed vertical lines in Figures 14.2 and 14.3 distinguish the three periods.

One way of measuring the level of compliance with the SAL is to observe the difference between these two lines. In particular, we expect budget actors to try to shift expenditures from SAL spending to spending not covered by the limit in an attempt to circumvent Proposition 4's intended effects. The figure shows what we predict in Chapter 3: In the first period, when compliance is not costly, the difference is more or less constant. As compliance becomes costlier in the second, we see a large increase in the

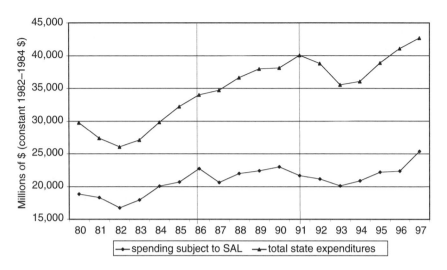

Figure 14.2   SAL Spending and Total Expeditures

amount of non-SAL spending relative to SAL spending. In the third period, when both costs and sanctions are low, the difference stabilizes and is once again relatively constant.

Our second measure of compliance is bonded indebtedness. Since both debt service and appropriations from voter-approved bonds are not subject to the SAL, the levels of state and local bonded indebtedness also reflect compliance with the SAL. We interpret increasing rates in the level of bonded indebtedness as reflecting attempts by policymakers to divert expenditures from items that are covered by the SAL to items that are exempt. Figure 14.3 shows levels of state and local debt. As expected, state debt is flat in the initial period, increases in the middle period, then levels off again in the third period.

Local debt is also flat in the first period and increases rapidly in the middle period. However, contrary to expectations, it continues to shoot upward in the third period when the costs of compliance with the SAL are relatively low. Although we only speculate on the reasons for this anomaly, we believe the continued upward trend suggests that local governments' budgets remained tightly constrained in the early and mid-1990s, leading them to shift spending to bonds. The constraints may stem in part from the SAL, but it is likely that they also result from lower local government revenues. In particular, Proposition 13 sharply curtailed local governments' abilities to raise taxes. As a result, revenue transfers from the state to local governments have become a primary source of local government's revenue. As the recession of the early 1990s cut state revenues and imposed difficult

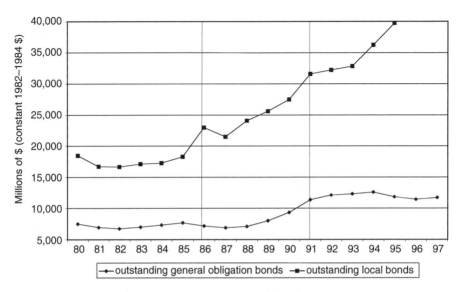

Figure 14.3   Bonded Indebtedness

budget decisions on the legislature and the governor, however, the state reduced these transfers and likely contributed to the increase in local debt that we see in the later years of Figure 14.3.

To summarize, we see compliance with the SAL provision of Proposition 4 varying as sanctions and compliance costs changed over time, where the nature of the changes is as Chapter 3 predicts.

EPILOGUE: TAXPAYER REFUNDS

It is interesting to compare compliance with the State Appropriations Limit provision of Proposition 4 to compliance with the initiative's taxpayer refund provision. The two provisions share many of the same features. For most of the period, the costs of complying with the taxpayer refund provision were minimal. In the early period, between 1980 and 1985, state revenues were far below the SAL and so no refunds were necessary. Similarly, in the period after 1991, the Proposition 111 raised the SAL, leaving the state in no danger of raising more revenues than allowed. In the period between 1986 and 1990, however, state revenues exceeded the SAL in one fiscal year, 1987–1988. In response, the state complied fully with Proposition 4's refund provision and returned $1.1 billion to taxpayers, in increments of $118 for individuals and $236 for married couples filing jointly.

One might ask why state government actors chose to comply fully with the taxpayer refund provision of Proposition 4 and only partially with the SAL provision. The difference, it appears, is that a majority of legislators and the governor both preferred full compliance with the taxpayer refunds. The prospect of mailing taxpayers checks—scheduled to arrive near the Christmas holiday—lead them to favor full compliance. It is also important to note, however, that public and elite response to the taxpayer refunds was not unanimously positive. Some people felt that the money would be better spent on cash-starved government programs such as education (see reference to the 1989 Field Poll above). Such sentiments fed support for and the ultimate passage of Proposition 98 of 1988, which guaranteed substantial state funding for K–14 education, and Proposition 111 of 1990, which eventually amended the SAL.

15

Public School Finance and the Limited Legacy of Proposition 13

The central premise of this book is that the effects of voter initiatives are often less severe than the initiatives' proponents intended. Public officials have many ways to move policy outcomes closer to ones they prefer. They can pass implementing legislation that either circumvents or undercuts an initiative. They can creatively interpret the language of an initiative, or, on occasion, simply pretend it isn't there.

In our final and most detailed case study, we extend the previous analysis by examining the impact of two initiatives, as well as a court-ordered mandate, that were *not* circumvented, but were instead implemented in a manner much as the authors of the measures intended. The policy area on which it focuses is public school finance, and the impact of Proposition 13 (1978), Proposition 4 (1979), and a series of decisions rendered by the California Supreme Court in favor of a plaintiff named *Serrano*. The book's appendix contains a comprehensive description of all of the data used in this case.

Our case study makes two central points. First, these initiatives and court decisions have been given far too much blame (or credit, depending on one's point of view) for subsequent conditions and events in California. Just because undesirable policy outcomes emerged in the years following passage of Propositions 13 and 4 and the *Serrano* decisions does not mean they were caused by either of the propositions or by the *Serrano* decisions. It is well-known in the social sciences that correlation does not establish causation, but neither does temporal order.

Second, rather than represent sharp reversals of policy, these voter-approved ballot measures and court decisions were consistent with ongoing trends in public policy. Though they amplify differences between California and the rest of the states in the country, Propositions 13 and 4 and *Serrano* did not create these differences. They were, to put it another way, policy choices that were flowing with, rather than against, the "current of history," to use Rosenberg's (1991) metaphor.

THE RECENT HISTORY OF PUBLIC SCHOOL FINANCE IN CALIFORNIA

We begin by describing trends in public school finance in California since 1969. Figure 15.1 shows how funding levels per pupil in California's public schools (K–12) compares to those of other states. These data, obtained from the National Center for Educational Statistics, are based on average daily attendance figures.[1]

Before the 1980s, California's expenditures per pupil were higher than the national average. Since then, they have fallen further and further behind the national norm. California ranked eighteenth among U.S. states in public school funding in 1975. Twenty years later, it ranked forty-first.

Most observers blame the long, downward trend in California's financial support for the state's public schools on two major changes in the state's fiscal environment. The first, an event that remains for many Californians the defining moment of their political lives, is the passage of Proposition 13 in 1978. Adopted as an amendment to the state constitution, this initiative rolled back property tax assessments dramatically, and capped future increases in property tax liabilities, in the absence of a sales-triggered reassessment, to no more than two percent per annum. A year later, California voters approved Proposition 4 (the Gann Initiative), which limited increases in state spending per capita to the minimum of either the rate of inflation or the percentage increase in personal income.

Many believe that the subsequent loss of state tax revenue resulting from these two initiatives led to a general underfunding of the public sector in California. In Schrag's (1998) dark vision of contemporary California, for

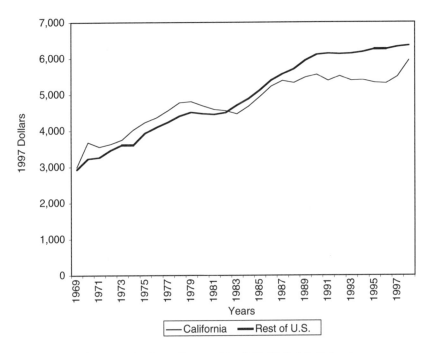

Figure 15.1   Spending per Pupil, K–12 Public Schools

example, much of what he believes has gone wrong in the Golden State stems directly from the "radical tax and spending limitations" (p. 65) imposed by Propositions 13 and 4. Or, as he puts it,

> The passage of Proposition 13 serves as a convenient way of dividing the post–World War II era in California between the postwar period of optimism, with its huge investment in public infrastructure and its strong commitment to the development of quality education systems and other public services, and a generation of declining confidence and shrinking public services (p. 10).

The second major development that has been seen to undermine the fiscal basis of support for public education in California is the equalization of expenditures mandated by the *Serrano* decisions. In the landmark case of *Serrano v. Priest* (1971), the California Supreme Court ruled that the then-existing funding system of public school finance, in which school districts relied largely upon local property taxes, was unconstitutional. The old system allowed wealthier districts to finance much higher levels of expenditures per pupil than poorer districts (see Coons, Clune, and Sugarman 1970). This, the Court ruled, violated the "fundamental right" that all children in the state had to a good public education. In *Serrano II* (1976) the

Court effectively ruled that local districts could not use any mechanism to increase funding that was wealth-based, and that cross-district disparities in expenditures per pupil could not exceed $100.

Legislation enacted in response to the *Serrano* decisions provides that all school districts in California (with the exception of a small number of wealthy districts) receive from the state whatever revenue is required to peg their spending per pupil at the same target level. By the mid-1980s, spending levels in nearly 95 percent of all school districts in California lay within the allowable band of variation, which, because of inflation, is currently about $300 (Rubinfeld 1995).

In the pre-*Serrano* system of educational finance, the desire for public schools that were better than (or at least as good as) those in neighboring, competing districts bolstered the willingness of voters to pay higher property taxes. Residents of wealthy districts were also assured that their property taxes would be spent in their own school districts. But public elementary and secondary education in California is now funded as if all students attend a single, statewide school district. In the post-*Serrano* era, therefore, some of the property taxes paid by residents in wealthy areas are, in effect, transferred to distant school districts. To be sure, poorer districts receive more funding than they would have under the pre-*Serrano* system, but some of the motive force supporting the old system—the willingness to pay higher property taxes to support local schools—has disappeared.

A number of studies have attempted to estimate whether the *Serrano* decision caused the twenty-year decline in expenditures per pupil. Silva and Sonstelie (1995) estimate that about half the decline in financial support for California's public schools relative to the rest of the country can be traced to *Serrano's* equal funding requirement. Fernandez and Rogerson (1997), using a similar public finance model, found that shifting from the old type of funding to a more equal *Serrano*-type of funding reduces overall spending by roughly 20 percent. A drop of this magnitude is fairly close to the difference in public school funding that currently exists between California and the national average.

The slide in California's ranking among the states in expenditures per pupil would seem to be yet another example of what Okun (1975) called the "big trade-off" between equality and efficiency. Making sure that everyone gets the same size piece of the pie can mean that people contribute less to the making of the pie, leaving a smaller pie left to split and smaller pieces for everyone. In discussing the *Serrano* case, Kozol (1991) thus concludes that although "...the plaintiffs won the equity they sought, it is to some extent a victory of losers" (p. 221).

Moreover, Fischel (1982) claims that the *Serrano* decisions, which effectively decoupled the linkage between local taxes and local school expenditures, "caused" Proposition 13—or at least made tax and expenditure limitations much more attractive to California voters. Careful studies of the

Tax Revolt era reveal no evidence of voters making such calculations (see especially Sears and Citrin 1982). Nevertheless, many people continue to argue that Propositions 13 and 4 and the *Serrano* decisions caused the erosion of expenditures per pupil in California schools.

Other studies contradict these accounts. Several studies, for example, suggest that the widely heralded tax limitation initiatives of the late 1970s and early 1980s had little lasting effect on state and local revenues or expenditures, either in California or in other states in which they were adopted (Rabushka and Ryan 1982; Gold 1988; Herbers 1990). This is primarily because the economic recovery that followed the 1981–82 recession was strong, leading state and local revenue and expenditure growth levels to return to pre-limitation levels. Moreover, Proposition 13 pertained only to the property tax. Since government actors can and do use other taxes, charges, and fees to compensate for losses of revenue from any single source, such as property taxes, it is thought that they can easily get around the intent of such limitations. Consider, for example, that state and local governments all over the country have successfully circumvented constitutional limitations on certain types of bonded indebtedness by issuing other forms of debt (see, for example, Kiewiet and Szakaly 1996).

Also weighing in against the idea that Propositions 13 and 4 and the *Serrano* decisions caused the decline of spending per pupil is the fact that many states have both higher public school expenditures and higher levels of equality than California (Hertert, Busch, and Odden 1994). Moreover, a recent study by Murray, Evans, and Schwab (1998) suggests that in the many states that have had court-ordered equality constraints imposed, overall expenditures on public schools have actually increased. They claim, for example, "Successful litigation reduced inequality by raising spending in the poorest districts while leaving spending in the richest districts unchanged, thereby increasing aggregate spending on education" (p. 789). Taken together, studies such as these provide reasons to doubt the common belief that Propositions 13 and 4 and the *Serrano* decisions caused the drop in spending per pupil.

IMPLEMENTATION OF PROPOSITION 13
AND THE SERRANO DECISIONS

Before investigating whether or not Propositions 13 and 4 and the *Serrano* decisions were as consequential for school funding as many have claimed, it is worthwhile to first consider the extent to which state government complied with these decisions.

Proposition 13 is a prime example of full and faithful implementation. In the days preceding its approval by the voters, Quinn (1978), writing in the *California Journal*, observed that the legislature and governor had at their disposal several "time-tested means of rendering initiatives inoperative" (p. 153). These included:

- the insertion of a more moderate alternative on the ballot to undercut support for the proposition (which was in fact done in the case of Proposition 13),
- a series of court appeals, which, as Quinn (1978) puts it, would cause "an initiative launched overwhelmingly by the voters [to] sink slowly into a sea of litigation, never to be seen again,"
- simply ignoring it, a ploy that had succeeded nicely on many previous occasions.

Proposition 13, however, did not fall to a more moderate alternative, get lost in the appeals process, or go away because people eventually lost interest. Why was this the case?

One reason the initiative was fully implemented is that it was very specific, making the ease of observing compliance high. More important, however, is the fact that policymakers who were empowered to implement and enforce the initiative either supported it or anticipated serious sanctions for failing to comply. Attorney General Evelle Younger, who was also the Republican nominee for governor in the impending November election, had supported passage of 13. He urged the California Supreme Court to move as expeditiously as possible in their review of the legal challenges that had been filed against it. As it turned out, Chief Justice Rose Bird and three other associate justices of the California Supreme Court were also on the ballot that November, a situation that may have militated against a state Supreme Court decision to overturn this highly popular initiative. The justices ruled quickly, upholding the legality of the proposition on all points save a relatively small section pertaining to the taxation of business inventories.

But most importantly, Governor Jerry Brown, facing a formidable electoral challenge from Younger, abandoned his previous opposition to the proposition and skillfully repositioned himself to become its patron saint. Vowing to faithfully carry out the will of the people, Brown cut his proposed budget, advocated and won a pay freeze for state employees, devised a plan to distribute the surplus in the state treasury, and developed the formula by which state monies would compensate local governments for property tax revenue shortfalls. Anticipating today's computer graphics technology, a celebrated cartoon of the time portrays Brown's visage morphing into that of Proposition 13 co-author Howard Jarvis (see Salzman 1978). Brown won re-election.

When we examine compliance with *Serrano*, a similar story emerges. Following the initial ruling of the California Supreme Court in 1971, state officials had many strategies available for overturning, circumventing, or at least indefinitely delaying the impact of the decision. One option was to place a referendum on the ballot that, if approved, would make the local property tax an acceptable source of school revenue—in other words, to make what the court had ruled unconstitutional explicitly constitutional.

Could such an initiative have won? Republicans might have favored it as a defense of local control, and urban Democrats might have supported it because their schools were likely to lose funding when *Serrano* was implemented. But what has been lost in the mist of time is an appreciation of the factors that generated large inequalities in school district tax bases. The tremendous disparities between poor communities such as Baldwin Park and wealthy areas such as Beverly Hills notwithstanding, it was the amount of commercial and industrial property, and not so much the price of residential real estate, that determined the relative wealth of California school districts. Schools in urban districts like San Francisco, Oakland, Los Angeles, and Long Beach were actually better funded before *Serrano* than many schools in suburban areas. With such caveats in mind, it is not at all clear that the constitutional move mentioned above would have succeeded.

The state also could have lodged any number of additional legal challenges to delay, perhaps indefinitely, implementation of the equal funding requirement. The record of school finance litigation in other states is instructive in this regard. In New Jersey, for example, the Supreme Court was continuing to rule on the constitutionality of its school finance system twenty years after rendering its initial decision (Murray, Evans, and Schwab 1998). Cases in other states remain pending today. As a result, even when states pass *Serrano*-like reforms, the effects can be modest (Dayton 1996; Bundt 1998). Dayton's (1996) assessment is striking in its resonance with the main theme of this book:

> Significant variation exists in the research and opinions reviewed, but many scholars have been pessimistic about the efficacy of judicial involvement in funding reform. A partial explanation for this pessimism may be unrealistic expectations about the role of the courts in the reform process. Funding reform requires legislative action, and under the United States system of constitutional governance courts may influence *but not control* legislative outcomes (p. 27, emphasis added).

In California, however, the state legislature, and governors Reagan and Brown, chose to implement the *Serrano* mandates rather than to resist them. The reasons for this choice are not difficult to understand. A Field Poll taken in August of 1978 revealed that Californians overwhelmingly supported the principle of equal funding. Over 90 percent supported equal expenditures per pupil, even when explicitly instructed that equalization would necessarily redistribute resources to poor districts and away from wealthy ones.

Popular accounts of the implementation of the *Serrano* financing scheme tend to portray compliance by the state as slow and grudging. It seems entirely unrealistic, however, to expect a change of this magnitude to occur quickly. By comparison to other states, California's implementation of funding equalization appears to have been relatively rapid and complete. In the session immediately following *Serrano v. Priest*, the state legislature adopted SB90, a measure that dramatically increased equalizing state assistance to local school districts. This legislation also capped the total amount of revenue per pupil (derived from both state and local sources) that a school district could raise. Further legislation to increase the rate at which spending equalization occurred was approved in 1977 following the 1976 *Serrano II* ruling, and again, following Proposition 13, in 1978. By the mid-1980s, spending levels in nearly 95 percent of all school districts in California lay within the allowable band of variation (Rubinfeld 1995).

THE FALL OF PER-PUPIL SPENDING IN CALIFORNIA

Having provided basic background information on California public school financing, we now turn to the central task of this study—to gauge how Propositions 13 and 4 and the *Serrano* decisions affected the state's public school spending patterns. In order to gain a full and accurate understanding of what has happened, it is important to do three things that have not been done systematically in previous studies.

First, the analysis must move beyond simple comparisons of per pupil spending levels and look at expenditures as a function of available taxable resources. Doing so is necessary to determine the extent to which variations in state school expenditures depend on variations in personal income both across states and over time.

Second, it is necessary to look not only at revenue and expenditure data in the years following these initiatives and court decisions, but also at these data in the decade or so preceding them. Taking such a broad perspective gives us a chance to determine whether the new policies caused changes in prior trends or merely reinforced what was happening before their passage.

Third, we must examine public school expenditures in the context of overall state spending. There are myriad other competing demands for each budget dollar; money spent on the public schools cannot be spent for other worthy purposes, and money spent for other worthy purposes cannot be spent on public schools. We thus need to determine how much money is allocated to public schools, in California and in the rest of the states, as a percentage of total spending by state and local governments.

Figure 15.2 displays spending per pupil in California, compared to the rest of the states, per thousand dollars of personal income per capita. It is,

Figure 15.2   Spending per Pupil/$1,000 per Capita Personal Income

roughly speaking, a measure of how much monetary "effort," given residents' incomes, that states put toward K–12 education. What the figure shows is similar to recent results by Fernandez and Rogerson (1998), who showed that in the U.S., expenditures per pupil on public education have closely tracked changes in personal income since 1950. Rather than the relative decline in support for public schools that is seen for California in Figure 15.1, the data in Figure 15.2 reveal instead a high degree of continuity in educational funding decisions.

To at least as far back as school year 1969, California, according to this measure, *has always spent a relatively smaller proportion of its residents' personal income on public education than have other states.* In fact, over the past 30 years California consistently ranked among the bottom handful of states in the proportion of personal income that government dedicates to public education. To be sure, the gap between California and the rest of the states increased over the next three decades. In the early years of the series, Californians tended to spend about 85 percent as much as other states when we control for personal income, but only about 75 percent as much by the end of it. In the analyses that follow, we will certainly consider the extent to which Propositions 13 and 4 and the *Serrano* decisions affected the increase in the size of the gap. The trend also implies, however, that any effects we might associate with these events simply increased the degree to which California lagged behind most other states before the *Serrano* decisions and the two propositions. In no way does this trend signal a sharp reversal of California's education funding policy relative to that of other states.

But if Californians have always spent a relatively smaller proportion of their personal income on public education, why the sharp, relative decline in expenditures per pupil evident in Figure 15.1? The answer is that it is possible to fall farther and farther behind other states if the others are growing while your state is standing still.

To assess the impact of Propositions 13 and 4 and *Serrano*, it is crucially important to take into account the slippage California has experienced in personal income levels (and thus in its tax base) relative to the other states. As the data in Figure 15.3 show, in 1968 personal income per capita in California was 21 percent higher than in the rest of the country. The relatively large tax base generated relatively high levels of public expenditures. Therefore, the California of 1968 was not unlike a wealthy school district under the pre-*Serrano* funding formula. It could devote a smaller share of its financial resources to K–12 education and still spend considerably more per pupil than the national average.

Over the next two decades, however, California's income advantage declined. At first it declined slowly. Later it declined rapidly, as the state

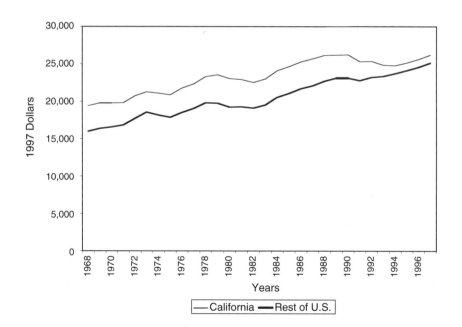

Figure 15.3   Real per Capita Income

slid into a severe recession in the early 1990s. By 1996, the per capita income advantage California enjoyed relative to the rest of the states in the country was a mere four percent.

To recap, through the later decades of the twentieth century California became increasingly average in terms of its tax base. What did not change over this same period is that *California persisted in lagging behind the rest of the country in the share of its tax base that its government devoted to public education.* Therefore, the affluent California of 1968 could devote a relatively smaller share of its resources to public schools and still outspend the rest of the country on a per pupil basis. The far less affluent California of 1995, devoting roughly the same share of resources to public schools, fell far below the national average in spending per pupil.[2]

Indeed, California's level of spending per pupil declined relative to other states from the late 1960s to the mid-1990s. This is not to say that income levels in California have fallen in absolute terms since 1968 (although they certainly did during the 1990–94 recession). It is rather that personal income per capita has grown less rapidly in California than in the rest of the states. Similarly, the fact that the rest of the states have, on average, nearly caught up with California in personal income per capita does not make California an unusual case. Since the end of World War II, income differentials across the various regions and states have narrowed considerably. Relative income gains in the South have been particularly dramatic. Whereas in 1968 personal income per capita in the states of the former Confederacy was about 75 percent of the national average, today it is over 90 percent. Much of California's relative decline in expenditures per pupil, then, results from the persistent allocation of less personal income to K–12 education in a state that is not nearly as rich as it used to be when compared to other states.

ANALYSIS

The reduction in California's income per capita, relative to other states, and the simultaneous decline in California's spending per pupil, relative to other states, does not imply that Propositions 13 and 4 and the *Serrano* decisions played no role in the decline. Indeed, the data charted in Figure 15.2 suggest that the gap between California and the rest of the states grew in the years following 1978. Were the propositions and court decisions the cause?

We begin our answer to this question with the fact that if the Propositions and *Serrano* decisions did negatively affect expenditures per pupil, they would have done so in different ways. Propositions 13 and 4 were not directed at public education specifically, but at state and local government in general. The way in which they would have reduced financial support for public schools, then, is by *limiting overall taxing and spending* by state and local governments.

The *Serrano* decisions, on the other hand, applied directly to public school finance. According to the critics, the equalization constraints these decisions imposed reduced many taxpayers' motives to support further increases in education spending—particularly those citizens who believed that they or their district would reap few of the benefits of the tax increases. If these critiques are true, then this change in public attitudes towards school funding would result in the public schools *receiving a smaller share* of state and local spending. Total state and local spending need not have been affected at all.

We continue our answer with the knowledge that the decisions were made at different times. Determining when the tax and expenditure limitations were put in place is easy. Proposition 13 passed in June 1978, and its provisions applied immediately to the next fiscal year, FY1979. (For all practical purposes, fiscal years and school years are equivalent). Proposition 4 was adopted in November 1979, and so was to take effect in fiscal year 1980. The course of litigation entailed by the *Serrano* decisions, on the other hand, runs from the first decision, rendered by the California Supreme Court in August 1971, through the final case (*Serrano IV*), decided in 1986 (Rubinfeld 1995). A review of the historical record reveals that the state legislature and Governor Ronald Reagan responded immediately to the initial 1971 judgment. In the legislative session of 1972, they adopted SB90, which dramatically increased equalizing state assistance to local school districts. We thus concur with Murray, Evans, and Schwab (1998) and identify the first school year after the initial decision, 1973, as the beginning of the post-*Serrano* period. This period ends, and the post-Proposition 13 and 4 period begins, in 1979.

With these facts in hand, we want to estimate:

1. The extent to which Propositions 13 and 4 reduced spending per pupil in California's public schools by limiting overall state and local spending.
2. The extent to which the *Serrano* decisions' equalization requirements reduced spending per pupil after 1973 by causing government actors to allocate a smaller share of total state and local spending to K–12 education.

We answer these questions by examining trends in total state and local government general expenditures and changes in the percentage of these expenditures allocated to education between 1969 and 1996 (the latest year for which such data were available to us when we began this study). We use a method of examination called *statistical regression analysis*. This technique allows us to sort out which of many factors, including Propositions 13 and 4 and the *Serrano* decisions, are most likely to have caused the decline in California's spending per pupil. Multiple regression analyses are devices that scientists and policy analysts use to sort out the individual effects of the many factors in the environment that could affect the thing that they are attempting to explain (which for us is per pupil spending patterns). In other words, multiple regression analyses allow a researcher to estimate the effect of a single factor, holding constant the potentially contaminating effect of other factors.

If, for example, scientists wanted to explain how heredity affects height, they would first gather data on height, heredity, diet, and other factors that are also suspected to affect how tall people are. Then they would run a regression whose point is to sort out how these factors actually correspond to height. If tall parents are more likely to have tall children, holding factors like diet constant, then the scientists would expect to see a large positive effect of heredity. If, by contrast, tall parents are more likely to have short children and vice versa, then the scientists would expect to see heredity have a negative effect. The *coefficients* that regression analyses produce are the analyst's estimate of how the named factor (heredity in the example above, Propositions 13 and 4 and *Serrano* in what follows) affects what we are attempting to explain (height in the example above, spending per pupil in what follows).[3]

In our regression analyses, we do not treat the propositions and the *Serrano* decisions as the only possible causes of changes in education spending per capita. We also include the following "usual suspects"—other factors that may affect spending, independent of the initiatives and court rulings:

- The percentage of school age children (i.e., between the ages of 5 and 17) in the state's population. Previous research indicates that spending on education tends not to fully adjust for gains and losses in enrollment (Fernandez and Rogerson 1988). It tends neither to grow quickly enough when enrollments increase, thus resulting in lower spending per pupil, nor to shrink quickly enough when enrollments fall, thus resulting in higher spending per pupil. These researchers attribute stickiness in educational spending to the lack of flexibility school districts have in hiring and firing teachers, and in either building or closing school buildings.
- The percentage of state population over the age of 65. Because their children are no longer in school, areas with more senior citizens may prefer relatively lower levels of spending on public schools.
- The crime rate, as measured by the Uniform Crime Report Index. Opponents of spending on jails and prisons frequently point out that it costs less money to send someone to Harvard for a year than it does to put him in San Quentin Prison. Whether or not one finds this a cogent argument, public safety and education undoubtedly place competing

claims on public dollars. States with high crime rates may thus spend relatively more on police, prisons, and criminal courts, and consequently relatively less on K–12 education.

* Real personal income per capita. As indicated previously, this has been shown to be strongly related to financial support for K–12 education (Fernandez and Rogerson 1998).

Again, the advantage of regression analysis is that it allows us to distinguish the effect of each of the usual suspects on spending per pupil from the effects of *Serrano* and the propositions.

In addition to the usual suspects, some of our regressions also include a battery of state-specific variables. These variables uncover how forces within a state that are not captured by the potential causes listed above affect spending per pupil.[4] Put another way, they show us the extent to which individual states differ from each other, holding constant the factors listed above. So, we can compare the coefficient labelled "California" to those of the other states to gauge just how far California lags behind the national norm in spending per pupil, controlling for the effects of the usual suspects.

Other regressions do not include these state-specific variables. They provide a second way of comparing California to other states. In these analyses, we inspect the regression's "residuals." These residuals reflect aspects of school spending that are not explained by the factors included in the regression analysis. If, on inspection of the residuals associated with our California data, we find a large negative residual, we gain evidence that spending per pupil in California was considerably lower than would otherwise be expected based on the factors listed above.

We report our first regression results in Table 15.1. The top number in each entry is the coefficient and the bottom number in parentheses is the standard error. If the coefficient is at least twice as large as the standard error, we follow standard scientific procedure and call it significant—which means that the coefficient is very unlikely to provide false information about whether the named factor has a positive or negative effect on spending.

As expected, personal income per capita has an extremely powerful effect upon spending per pupil. Coefficients for the effects of crime rates and the percentage of a state's population between ages 5 and 17 are also quite large, have the expected directional effect, and are significant. Contrary to our expectations, however, states with relatively large cohorts of senior citizens tend to spend more on public education, not less.

Remarkably, the record of California in supporting K–12 education looks even worse here than in Figures 15.1 and 15.2. In the first equation, the California coefficient was smaller than that of any other state except Florida. The difference between the coefficient for California (664) and the

Table 15.1   Regression Analysis, per-Pupil Funding of K–12 Education in California, SY 1969–98

Variable	Per-Pupil Expenditures	Expenditures/Personal Income
Personal Income	.259	—
	(.008)	—
Crime Rate	−.046	−.0015
	(.017)	(.066)
Percent 5–17	−124.4	−.667
	(9.8)	(.039)
Percent Over 65	88.8	.372
	(18.4)	(.083)
Other States (average)	1709	.341
California	664	.292
	(472)	(.018)
California Rank	48	47
Observations	1469	1469
R^2 (adj.)	.94	.82

average for the other states (1709) indicates that during this 30-year period, spending per pupil was over a thousand (1997) dollars lower than would otherwise be predicted for U.S. states in general. Results associated with the second equation, which measures spending per pupil as a percentage of real personal income per capita, are very similar. The ratio of expenditures per pupil to personal income per capita during this time period was considerably lower in California than in the rest of the states.

Figures 15.4 and 15.5 plot the residuals from regression equations in which the state-specific variables were omitted. The overall pattern is very similar to those just described. In both equations, *all* residuals for California are large and negative, indicating that in no year did spending per pupil climb as high as it would have been in other states if they resembled California in terms of the population characteristics listed above.

When we subdivide the results into the pre-*Serrano*, post-*Serrano*, and post-Propositions 13 and 4 periods, however, some important differences arise. First, the residuals for California were smaller in the post-*Serrano* period (SY1973–78) than in prior years. In the first equation, they averaged −634 in the latter period compared to −761 in the former. In the second equation, they declined from −.033 on average to −.024. In other words, the state actually performed *worse* in the pre-*Serrano* period, in spending per

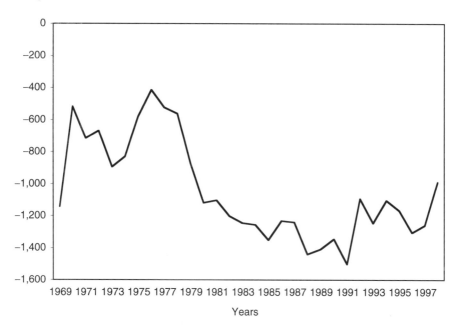

Figure 15.4   Residuals for California from the per-Pupil Expenditures Regression

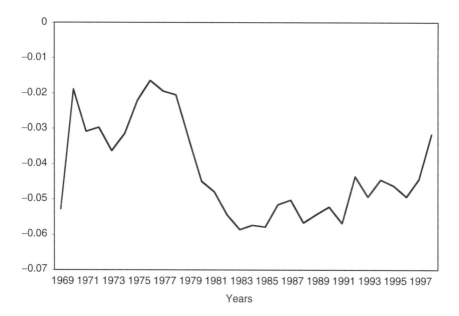

Figure 15.5   Residuals for California for the Expenditures/Personal Income
Regression

pupil, when compared to other states. We test the "*Serrano* caused the decline" hypothesis more directly below, but at this point our results provide no evidence that the equalization constraints imposed by the California Supreme Court depressed funding for public schools.

In the years following passage of Propositions 13 and 4, in contrast, the residuals in both equations grew considerably larger. In the period beginning in 1979, they averaged a whopping −1225 in the first equation and −.049 in the second. In short, the extent to which expenditures per pupil in California fell below the national norm was considerably greater in the years following passage of Propositions 13 and 4.

We now turn to the main task of this analysis, which is to determine whether this slippage can reasonably be attributed to the passage of Propositions 13 and 4 or to the *Serrano* decisions. One hypothesis is that between 1973 and 1978, the spending equalization constraints imposed by the *Serrano* decisions reduced spending per pupil because it led to K–12 education receiving a smaller share of total state and local spending. A second hypothesis is that beginning in 1979, Propositions 13 and 4 reduced spending per pupil in California's public schools by limiting overall state and local spending.

Looking first at trends in total state and local general expenditures, we see in Figure 15.6 that, as a percentage of personal income, overall spending in California has never differed a great deal from the average of the other states. There is in this figure, however, some evidence of the impact of Propositions 13 and 4. Before their passage, California was a bit higher in overall expenditures than the rest of the states, but it was somewhat lower in the years following. From about 1983 onward, however, the difference between California and the rest of the states steadily narrowed and it had disappeared completely by 1996. It was during this same time frame that expenditures per pupil were falling relative to the rest of the states. At this juncture, then, the evidence suggests that while Propositions 13 and 4 may have caused a temporary decline in overall expenditures relative to other states, they do not seem to be the reason that public school expenditures per pupil in California continue to lag behind on other states.

In contrast, the data in Figure 15.7 indicate that California has consistently differed from other states in the percentage of state and local spending allocated to K–12 education. Year in and year out, public schools have received a comparatively small piece of the pie. This was true before the *Serrano* decisions as well as after them.

In fact, the difference between California and other states actually narrowed some during the 1970s, which is exactly the opposite of what a "*Serrano* caused the decline" hypothesis would predict. The difference narrowed again in the late 1980s as well, but subsequently widened again. Overall, in most years during the last three decades, the share of total state and local expenditures devoted to K–12 education has been about three to

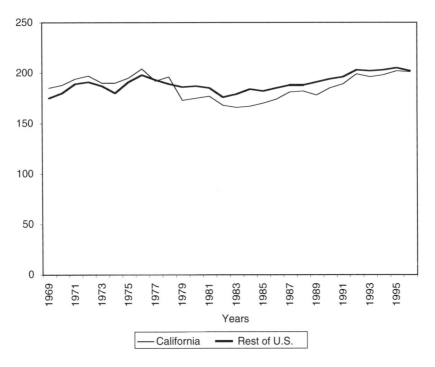

Figure 15.6   Total Expenditures per $1,000 Personal Income

four percent lower in California than the average of the other states. Thus, it appears unlikely that *Serrano* caused this difference.

We next take a more careful look at the data on general expenditures and on the percentage of expenditures allocated to K–12 education, again running multiple regression analyses. The results, reported in Table 15.2, indicate that we were not misled by the raw data plotted in Figures 15.6 and 15.7. Looking first at the regression of total general expenditures/personal income, we see that the difference between the coefficient for California and the average of the other states is –.006, which is to say approximately zero. Its rank of twenty-ninth also implies that during this period the state has been very average in its overall level of state and local spending.

This is not the case for the share of spending allocated to elementary and secondary education. Here the .226 coefficient for California is .036 lower than the average for the other states, earning it a rank of 45 out of 49. This means that from 1969 to 1996, the percent of total state and local spending allocated to public schools in California, controlling for all the other factors specified above, has been nearly four percent less than other states.[5]

The same patterns emerge more clearly when we run regressions without the state-specific variables and inspect the residuals associated with

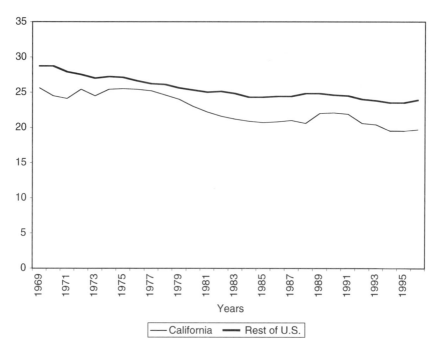

Figure 15.7 Spending on Elementary and Secondary Education as a Percentage of Total State and Local Government Expenditures

California. In Figure 15.8, which plots these residuals, we see that before the passage of Propositions 13 and 4, the percentage of personal income that flowed into state and local government expenditures was very close to what the regression would predict of U.S. states in general. The residuals became large and negative in fiscal year 1979, however, and finally bottomed out in fiscal year 1983. This constitutes clear support for the first hypothesis: Propositions 13 and 4 reduced spending per pupil in California's public schools by limiting state and local spending across the board. From then on, however, the residuals began moving in a sharply positive direction. By 1987, they were less than −.01, and from 1991 on they are positive—indicating more state and local spending than the regression equation would predict for U.S. states in general.

As we observed previously, it was during this same period that expenditures per pupil in California began to fall precipitously relative to the rest of the states. The consequences of Propositions 13 and 4 on overall expenditures, in short, had largely dissipated within seven years of their passage. They cannot be blamed for the sharp relative decline in spending per pupil that occurred after that. As we indicated earlier, what surely was responsi-

Table 15.2   Regression Analysis, Total General Expenditures and Percent
Allocated to K–12 Education, SY 1969–96

Variable	Total General Expenditure/Personal Income	Percent Allocated to K–12 Education
Personal Income	.016	.009
	(.003)	(.004)
Crime Rate	.004	−.0013
	(.005)	(.007)
Percent 5–17	.329	.290
	(.033)	(.042)
Percent Over 65	.644	−.711
	(.006)	(.080)
Other States (average)	−.004	.262
California	−.010	.226
	(.016)	(.021)
California Rank	29	45
Observations	1372	1372
R^2 (adj.)	.80	.74

ble for this slide was California's decline from a very affluent state, in terms of personal income per capita, to a very average state.

The residuals plotted in Figure 15.9 reinforce the patterns observed in Figure 15.7. Although all residuals are negative, they shrank from an average −.023 prior to the *Serrano* decision to a mere −.009 in the six years following. This is consistent both with Murray, Evans, and Schwab's (1998) recent findings, and also with a review of the historical record; as indicated previously, the legislative response to the 1971 decision, SB90 adopted in 1972, increased equalizing assistance from the state to local school districts, thus increasing total school spending substantially. Contrary to the "*Serrano* caused the decline" hypothesis, then, the equalization constraints imposed by *Serrano* corresponded to an increase rather than a decrease in the proportion of total state and local spending allocated to public schools.

The most dramatic movement in the residuals plotted in Figure 15.9 is from 1990 on, when they fall from about −.01 to −.045. By 1996, then, K–12 education was allocated about 4.5 percent less of total state and local spending than the regression equation would predict for U.S. states in general. This period coincides with California's slide into a long, severe recession. Spending on public education in California thus appears to be treated as

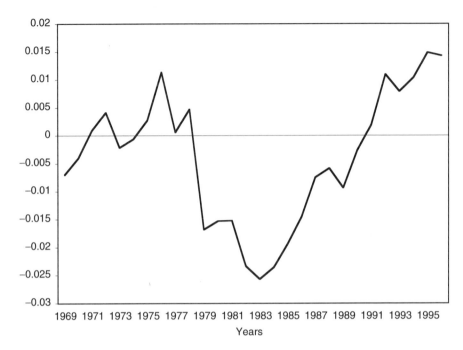

Figure 15.8   Residuals for California from the Total General Expenditures
Regression

something of a luxury good: during periods of budgetary stringency, not
only does the size of the fiscal pie shrink, but education gets an increasingly
smaller share of what is left.

SUMMARY

The passage of Propositions 13 and 4 clearly had a negative effect on expenditures per pupil in California. The effect, however, was indirect in that the
propositions' main effect was to constrain state and local government
spending in general, rather than education spending in particular. This effect, however, had largely dissipated by the mid-1980s. Therefore, the
sharp, relative decline in spending per pupil in the public schools of California that has occurred since then cannot be directly attributed to a tax revolt
that took place twenty years ago. Indeed, while California was catching up
to the national average in total expenditures as a percentage of personal income, it was falling further and further behind on education spending per
pupil.

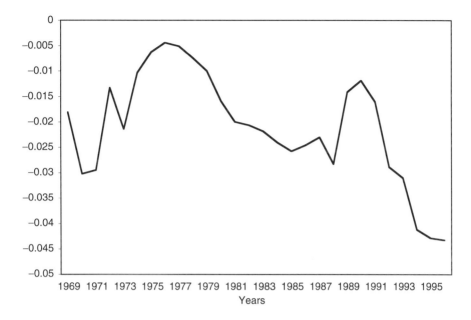

Figure 15.9 Residuals for California from the Allocation to Education Regression

State Supreme Court decisions mandating equal expenditures per pupil across school districts are also not the cause of the decline. All indications are that the *Serrano* decisions actually led to a larger share of total spending being allocated to elementary and secondary education.

Observed declines are instead the consequence of a state that has grown significantly less affluent relative to the other states in the country and that persists in allocating a smaller share of its budgetary resources to public schools. This is true before and after Proposition 13, before and after the *Serrano* decisions.

Finally, we should note, there have been significant increases in funding per pupil in California over the last few years. Given how far California had fallen below the average of other states, however, a significant gap still remains. Low funding levels translate into deferred maintenance, reduced extracurricular activities, the retention of old, outmoded textbooks, and little or no access to the Internet. Lower expenditures also necessitate larger class sizes. In 1995, there were 23.1 pupils enrolled per teacher in California public schools, a ratio surpassed only by Utah. Despite recent initiatives to reduce class sizes in the lower grades, public school classrooms in California remain some of the most crowded in the nation. For those concerned with educational quality, this is particularly troubling. Although the statistical association between public school expenditures and student performance is tenuous, there is evidence that students learn better in smaller classes (Krueger 1997).

For people concerned about these consequences, we now have an accurate accounting for why expenditures per pupil in California fell significantly below the national norm. What we do not have is an answer for why California has consistently allocated a smaller share of its financial resources to its public schools than have most other states.

NOTES

1. By "rest of the U.S.," we mean the average public school expenditure in all other states except Alaska. Alaska, because of its dependence on natural resource revenues, has a public finance regime that is fundamentally different from that of the other states, so it is almost always excluded in analyses of state and local policymaking.
2. The good news today, of course, is that the last few years have witnessed substantial gains in income growth, and expenditures per pupil have risen correspondingly. If present budgetary trends continue, California should be back to the national average in expenditures per pupil within a few years.
3. To learn more about multiple regression, see any college-level statistics textbook.
4. Because we include such a variable for every state, the equation is estimated without a constant term.
5. If California has perennially devoted a smaller share of total state and local spending to public education, relatively larger shares of spending must have flowed to other governmental goods and services. Ellwood (n.d.) reports that there are several areas in which California has consistently spent disproportionately more, as a function of personal income, than the national average. These include health and hospitals, welfare, natural resources, and public safety (police, fire, corrections). A similar pattern emerges if one looks at these areas of spending as percentages of total state and local spending.

16

Conclusion

The main lesson of *Stealing the Initiative* is that initiatives do not implement or enforce themselves. All initiatives require government actors to implement and enforce them. As a result, all initiatives grant government actors some discretion over how to comply with what the proponents wrote down in their initiative. Features of the political environment, such as the preferences of political actors and the resources an initiative's proponents can mobilize to punish noncompliance, are important in determining the extent to which initiatives will have the effect that their proponents' envisioned. Features of the economic environment, as seen in our case study of Proposition 13, can have similar effects. Features of the initiative itself, such as the specificity of its directions to government actors, the technical and political costs of compliance that it imposes, and the number of actors that compliance requires, are also important. Our case studies illustrate how attention to these factors allows us to understand better the wildly varying post-election fates of recent California initiatives.

From an initiative proponent's perspective, it would seem that our analysis has an obvious implication—to ensure greater compliance with one's winning initiative, simply write a measure that is clearer in its instructions about implementation and enforcement and find a credible way to sanction government actors who do not comply. We contend, however, that the solution for initiative proponents is not so simple. There are a number of reasons why it may be difficult to write such an initiative. For example, initiative proponents may lack the expertise necessary to specify the exact steps required to change policy. Or an initiative's policy consequences may be difficult to anticipate, requiring government actors to retain discretion in order to adapt its implementation and enforcement activities over time. Some policies require the actions of many actors and so implementation and enforcement decisions cannot be centralized. Finally, some activities are inherently difficult to monitor.

In addition to the inherent difficulties in writing precise initiative legislation, there is also a political reason that may prevent initiative proponents from seeking to increase compliance by wording their initiative precisely. The reason is the trade-off between an initiative's specificity and its ability to win an electoral majority. Highly specific initiatives are easy to criticize—more details imply a larger number of targets for opponent attacks. Initiative proponents can and do avoid criticism by couching their proposed policy changes in vague or ambiguous terms. Similarly, potential opponents may go along with a vague initiative knowing that their allies in state government will be able to reinterpret those provisions at the compliance stage. Thus, some initiative proponents may have no choice but to write an initiative in vague or ambiguous language. This may be their only way to obtain victory at the ballot box.

It is clear that government actors retain a great deal of discretion over what happens to initiatives after they pass. Given the severity of the requirements for full compliance, it is safe to assume that government actors exert at least some discretion over most winning initiatives. Therefore, the policy impact of most initiatives reflects a compromise between what electoral majorities and government actors want. This outcome is not all that dissimilar to the effect of the most influential public opinion polls.

What do our results imply about the initiative process itself? For people who think groups should be able to pass laws by initiative without the intervention of other government actors, our results should represent a cause for concern. For people who think that participation by state government actors results in better or more representative policies, our findings should be a cause for optimism.

Appendix

Additional Information about the Data

Data on expenditure figures per pupil are from the National Center for Education Statistics in the Department of Education. For school years 1970, 1980, 1981, and 1986–96, these data are taken from the *1998 Digest of Education Statistics*, available online in the NCES electronic catalog at *http://nces.ed.gov/pubsearch*. Data for SY1997 were obtained from "Revenues and Expenditures for Public Elementary and Secondary Education: School Year 1996–97," and for SY1998 from "Public Elementary and Secondary Education Statistics, Revised: School Year 1997–98." Both reports are also available from the NCES website. Data for all other years were taken from hard copy issues of the *Digest of Education Statistics*, with the following exceptions: (1) the entry for Florida for AY1974 was updated with the figure reported in Table 214 of the 1975 Statistical Abstract of the United States (hereafter SAUS), p. 130; (2) the entry for Montana for AY1973 was updated with the figure reported in Table 201 of the 1973 SAUS, p. 128. No data on per-pupil spending could be obtained for Montana for SY1972.

For SY1969–96, all per-pupil figures are calculated on an average daily attendance (ADA) basis. For SY1997 and SY1998, however, the only figures available are based upon fall enrollment, which is always larger than ADA.

111

To make these data as comparable as possible, they were multiplied by the ratio of fall enrollment to ADA figures for SY1996 (the last year for which both figures were available).

Estimates of state population and of selected age cohorts for 1970–79 are taken from "Intercensal Estimates of the Resident Population of the States 1970–80." For 1980–89 they are taken from "Resident Population for Selected Age Groups: 1980 to 1989," and for 1990–97 from "Estimates of the Population of the U.S. Regions, and States by Selected Age Groups and Sex: Annual Time Series, July 1, 1990 to July 1, 1997." These reports are available at *http://www.census.gov/population/estimates*, the Bureau of the Census's Web site. For 1968 and 1969 these data are taken from the Bureau of the Census's *Current Population Reports*, Series P-25, no. 437. The data for 1969 did not report separate 0–4 and 5–17 age cohorts, but only a 0–17 cohort. To obtain an estimate for the 5–17 cohort, we first calculated for years 1968 and 1970 the percentage of the 0–17 cohort constituted by the 5–17 cohort. In every state, this percentage was larger in 1970 and 1968, reflecting the impact of the baby boom moving through the age structure of the population. We then took the average of these two percentages and multiplied the 0–17 cohort figures for 1969 by it, thus generating an estimate for the 5–17 cohort.

Crime Rates for 1968 through 1995 are taken from *State Crime Data, 1960–96*, compiled by the Bureau of Justice Statistics, U.S. Department of Justice. These data are derived from the Federal Bureau of Investigation's annual *Uniform Crime Reports*, and can be downloaded from *http://www.ojp.usdoj.gov/bjs/datast.htm*. Data for 1996–1997 come from Table 4, Index of Crime: Region, Geographic Division, and State, 1996–1997, in *Uniform Crime Reports for the United States 1997*, published by the Federal Bureau of Investigation, available at *http://www.fbi.gov/ucr/Cius 97/97crime/97crime2.pdf*. These data are based upon state population estimates that may vary slightly from the most current estimates produced by the Bureau of the Census.

The Bureau of Economic Analysis's most recent estimates of state-level personal income data for 1968–97 can be downloaded from their Web site, which is located at *http://www.bea.doc.gov/bea/regional/spi/recent.htm*.

Consumer price index data for both calendar and academic year for years 1968–96 are taken from Table 38, Gross domestic product deflator, Consumer Price Index, education price indexes, and federal budget composite deflator: 1919 to 1997, which is available at *http://nces.ed.gov/pubs/digest97/d97t038.html*. For 1997 (SY1998) these figures were obtained from the Bureau of Labor Statistics' Web site.

References

Ainsworth, Bill. 1996. "Lawmakers Gain New Power to Alter Initiatives." *The Recorder*, December 17, 1996.

Baker, Bob. 1990. "Cal-OSHA Not Doing Its Job, Critics Charge." *Los Angeles Times*, January 25, 1990.

Booth, William. 1998. "In California Classrooms, a Troubled Transition." *Washington Post*, August 4, 1998.

Bowen, Frank M. and Eugene C. Lee. 1979. "Limiting State Spending: The Legislature or the Electorate" Research Report. Institute of Governmental Studies, University of California, Berkeley, CA.

Bowler, Shaun, and Todd Donovan. 1998. *Demanding Choices: Opinion, Voting, and Direct Democracy*. Ann Arbor: University of Michigan Press.

Braun, Gerry. 1987. "Spanish-Language Voting Materials May Bring Landmark Proposition 63 Lawsuit." *San Diego Union-Tribune*, January 31, 1987.

Bundt, Julie. 1998. "Winning in Court: Unsatisfactory Victories." Paper delivered at the Annual Meeting of the Midwest Political Science Association, Chicago, IL.

Cain, Bruce E., and Roger G. Noll. 1995. "Principles of State Constitutional Design." *Constitutional Reform In California: Making State Government More Effective and Responsive*, ed. Bruce E. Cain and Roger G. Noll. Berkeley: Institute of Governmental Studies Press.

California Bureau of Criminal Statistics. 1993. *Crime and Delinquency in California for all California Counties*. Sacramento: California Department of Justice, Division of Law Enforcement, Bureau of Criminal Statistics.

California Citizens Budget Commission. 1995. *Reforming California's Budget Process*. Los Angeles: Center for Governmental Studies.

California Department of Education. 1999. *http://165.74.253.12/webdev/index.html/htdocs/cilbranch/bien/bien.htm*

California Fair Political Practices Commission. 1978–1998. "Summary of Receipts and Expenditures by Committees Primarily Formed to Qualify, Support, or

Oppose a State Ballot Measure." 1978–1998 Primary and General Elections. Sacramento: California Fair Political Practices Commission.

California Governor. 1993. *Governor's Budget, 1993–1994*. Sacramento: Governor's Office.

California Secretary of State. 1978–1998. *Statement of the Vote*. Sacramento: Secretary of State.

California Secretary of State. 1996a. *http://www.ss.ca.gov/prd/bmc96/summprop198.htm*.

California Secretary of State. 1996b. *http://www.primary96.ca.gov*.

California Secretary of State. 1999. *http://www.ss.ca.gov*.

Coons, John, William Clune, and Stephen D. Sugarman. 1970. *Private Wealth and Public Education*. Cambridge: Harvard University Press.

Carson, Daniel C. 1987. "Other-Language Ballots OK, Van de Kamp Says." *San Diego Union-Tribune*, March 22, 1987.

Coye, Molly Joel. 1992. "Stop the Addiction: Adjusting to State's Budget Woes Shouldn't Send Anti-Smoking Success Up in Smoke." *San Diego Union-Tribune*, February 18, 1992, sec. B.

Dayton, John. 1996. "Examining the Efficacy of Judicial Involvement in Public School Finance Reform." Journal of Education Finance 22:1–27.

Deverell, William, and Tom Sitton. 1994. *California Progressivism Revisited*. Berkeley: University of California Press.

Dubois, Philip, and Floyd F. Feeney. 1992. *Improving the California Initiative Process: Options for Change*. Berkeley: California Policy Seminar.

Ellwood, John. N.d. "Alternatives for California's Future." *California Fiscal Reform: A Plan for Action*. Berkeley, CA: California Business–Higher Education Forum.

Ellwood, John W., and Mary Sprague. 1995. "Options for Reforming the California State Budget Process." *Constitutional Reform In California: Making State Government More Effective and Responsive*, ed. Bruce E. Cain and Roger G. Noll. Berkeley: Institute of Governmental Studies Press.

Federal News Service. 1998. Prepared statement of Joseph M. Farley, Ed.D., Representing the Oceanside Unified School District, Oceanside, California, Before the House Education and the Workforce Committee. June 24, 1999.

Fernandez, Raquel, and Richard Rogerson. 1997. "Educational Finance Reform and Investment in Human Capital." Paper presented at the Conference on Law and Federalism, Federal Reserve Bank of Minneapolis.

Fernandez, Raquel, and Richard Rogerson. 1998. "The Determinants of Public Education Expenditures: Evidence from the States, 1950–1990." Manuscript, New York University.

Field Institute. 1989. *Field (California) Poll*, #8901. [machine-readable data files] San Francisco, CA: The Field Institute [producer]. Berkeley, CA: University of California Data Archive [distributor].

Field Institute. 1994. *California Opinion Index*, vol. 4 (August). San Francisco: Field Institute.

Field Institute. 1997. *California Opinion Index*, vol. 5 (September). San Francisco: Field Institute.

Field Institute. 1999. *The Field Poll*, #1921. San Francisco: Field Institute.

Fischel, William. 1989. "Did *Serrano* Cause Proposition 13?" *National Tax Journal* 42:465–73.

Gerber, Elisabeth R. 1999. *The Populist Paradox: Interest Group Influence and the Promise of Direct Legislation*. Princeton: Princeton University Press.

Gerber, Elisabeth R., and Arthur Lupia. 1995. "Campaign Competition and Policy Responsiveness in Direct Legislation Elections." *Political Behavior* 17:287–306.

Gerber, Elisabeth R., Arthur Lupia, and Mathew D. McCubbins. N.d. "How State Government Responds to Voter Mandates: A Formal Model. Typescript: University of California, San Diego.

Gilliam, Jerry. 1987. "Bill Making English-Only Suits Harder to File Dies in Assembly." *Los Angeles Times*, June 5, 1987.

Gold, Steven. 1988. "The Tax Revolt 10 Years Later." *State Legislatures* 14:14–17.

Gorman, Siobhan. 1999. "A Bilingual Recess." *National Journal*, January 30, 1999.

Herbers, John. 1990. "Read My Lips: The Tax Revolt Hasn't Had All That Much Impact." *Governing* 4:11.

Hertert, Linda, Carolyn Busch, and Allan Odden. 1994. "School Financing Inequities Among the States: The Problem from a National Perspective." *Journal of Education Finance* 19:231–55.

Ingram, Carl. 1986. "Proposition 63 Backers Against Bilingual Education." *Los Angeles Times*, November 24, 1986.

Just Say No to Tobacco Dough Campaign, Case History. All materials pertaining to this case were provided by Gwilliam, Ivary, Chiosso, Cavalli, and Brewer (counsel for the plaintiffs), of Oakland, California.

Justice Policy Institute. 1999. *Striking Out: The Failure of California's "Three Strikes and You're Out" Law*. San Francisco: Justice Policy Institute.

Kiewiet, D. Roderick. 1995. "Constitutional Limitations on Indebtedness: The Case of California." *Constitutional Reform In California: Making State Government More Effective and Responsive*, ed. Bruce E. Cain and Roger G. Noll. Berkeley: Institute of Governmental Studies Press.

Kiewiet, D. Roderick, and Mathew D. McCubbins. 1991. *The Logic of Delegation: Congressional Parties and the Appropriations Process*. Chicago: University of Chicago Press.

Kiewiet, D. Roderick, and Kristin Szakaly. 1996. "Constitutional Limitations on Borrowing: An Analysis of State Bonded Indebtedness." *Journal of Law, Economics, and Organization* 12: 62–97.

Kimball Petition Management. 1997. Telephone interview.

Kozol, Jonathan. 1991. *Savage Inequalities: Children in America's Schools*. New York: Crown Publishers.

Krueger, Alan. 1997. "Experimental Estimates of Education Production Functions." Working Paper 379, Industrial Relations Section, Princeton University.

Legislative Analyst's Office. 1990. *The California Budget Process: Problems and Options for Change*. Sacramento: Legislative Analyst's Office.

Lowenstein, Daniel. 1982. "Campaign Spending and Ballot Propositions: Recent Experience, Public Choice Theory, and the First Amendment." *UCLA Law Review* 29:505–641.

Lupia, Arthur. 1992. "Busy Voters, Agenda Control, and the Power of Information." *American Political Science Review* 86:390–403.

Lupia, Arthur. 1994. "Shortcuts Versus Encyclopedias: Information and Voting Behavior in California Insurance Reform Elections." *American Political Science Review* 88: 63–76.

Lupia, Arthur, and Mathew D. McCubbins. 1998. *The Democratic Dilemma: Can Citizens Learn What They Need to Know?* New York: Cambridge University Press.

Lupia, Arthur, and Richard Johnston. 2000. "Are Voters to Blame? Voter Competence and Elite Maneuvers in Public Referendums." In *Referendum Democracy: Citizens, Elites, and Deliberation in Referendum Campaigns,* ed. Matthew Mendelsohn and Andrew Parkin. New York: Macmillan.

Magleby, David B. 1984. *Direct Legislation: Voting on Ballot Propositions in the United States.* Baltimore: Johns Hopkins University Press.

Miller, Kenneth P. 1999. "The Role of Courts in the Initiative Process: A Search for Standards." Paper delivered at the 1999 Annual Meeting of the American Political Science Association, Atlanta.

Mowry, George E. 1976. *The California Progressives.* Chicago: Quadrangle Books.

Murray, Sheila, William Evans, and Robert Schwab. 1998 "Education-Finance Reform and the Distribution of Education Resources." *American Economic Review* 88:789–812.

Noll, Roger G. 1995. "Executive Organization: Responsiveness vs. Expertise and Flexibility." In *Constitutional Reform In California: Making State Government More Effective and Responsive,* ed. Bruce E. Cain and Roger G. Noll. Berkeley: Institute of Governmental Studies Press.

Owens, John R., and Larry L. Wade. 1986. "Campaign Spending on California Ballot Propositions, Trends and Effects, 1924–1984." *Western Political Quarterly* 36:675–89.

Okun, Arthur. 1975. *Equality vs. Efficiency: The Big Tradeoff.* Washington, DC: The Brookings Institution.

Pressman, Jeffrey L., and Aaron Wildavsky. 1979. *Implementation* 3rd ed. Berkeley, CA: University of California Press.

Quinn, Tony. 1978. "The Specter of 'Black Wednesday:' How the Establishment Destroys Unwanted Initiatives Like Jarvis." *California Journal* 9:153–4.

Rabushka, Alvin, and Pauline Ryan. 1982. *The Tax Revolt.* Stanford: The Hoover Institution.

Rosenberg, Gerald. 1994. *The Hollow Hope.* Chicago: University of Chicago Press.

Rubinfeld, Daniel. 1995. "California Fiscal Federalism: A School Finance Perspective." Bruce Cain and Roger Noll, (eds.), *Constitutional Reform in California.* Berkeley, CA: University of California Press.

Salzman, Ed. 1978. "Life After Jarvis." *California Journal* 9:264–7.

San Diego City Schools. 1998. "Status Report on Implementation of Proposition 227." November 24, 1998. San Diego: San Diego City Schools.

San Diego Union-Tribune. 1987. "Foreign-Language Ballots OK, Attorney General Says." *San Diego Union-Tribune,* May 22, 1987.

San Francisco Examiner. 1998. "Bilingual Backers Sue to Halt 227." *San Francisco Examiner,* June 3, 1998.

San Francisco Unified School District. 1998. "SF Schools to Maintain Bilingual Programs." San Francisco Unified School District news release, June 3, 1998 (*http://www.sfusd.k12.us/news/prop227.html*).

Schnaiberg, Lynn. 1999. "Calif.'s Year on the Bilingual Battleground." *Education Week,* June 2, 1999.

Schrag, Peter. 1998. *Paradise Lost: California's Experience, America's Future.* Berkeley, CA: University of California Press.

Sears, David, and Jack Citrin. 1982. *Tax Revolt: Something for Nothing in California.* Cambridge: Harvard University Press.

Silva, Fabio, and Jon Sonstelie. 1995. "Did *Serrano* Cause a Decline in School Spending?" *National Tax Journal* 48:199–215.

Syer, John C., and John H. Culver. 1992. *Power and Politics in California*, 4th ed. New York: Macmillan.

Traitel, Dee Anne. "Activists Fight to Save Anti-Smoking Funds." *San Diego Union-Tribune*, April 13, 1992, sec. B.

Weinstein, Henry. 1988. "State to Restore Cal/OSHA in Response to Prop. 97 Approval." *Los Angeles Times*, November 30, 1988.

Weintraub, Daniel M. "Wilson Broke Law by Halting Anti-Smoking Campaign." *Los Angeles Times*, April 25, 1992, sec. A.

COURT CASES CITED

American Lung Association v. Wilson. 1996. 51 Cal. App. 4th 743.

Americans for Non-Smokers' Rights v. State of California. 1996. 51 Cal. App. 4th 724.

Bates v. Jones. 1997. 131 F.3d 843.

Garcia v. Superior Court of Orange County. 1997. 14 Cal. 4th 953.

Legislature of the State of California v. March Fong Eu. 1991. 54 Cal. 3d 492.

People v. Benson. 1998. 18 Cal. 4th 24.

People v Bermudez. 1996. 46 Cal. App. 4th 1618.

People v. Deloza. 1998. 18 Cal. 4th 585.

People v. Fuhrman. 1997. 16 Cal. 4th 930.

People v. Hazelton. 1996. 14 Cal. 4th 101.

People v. Superior Court (Roam). 1999. 69 Cal. App. 4th 1220.

People v. Superior Court (Romero). 1996. 13 Cal. 4th 497.

Serrano v. Priest. 1971. 5 Cal. 3d 587: 487 P. 2d 1241.

Serrano(II) v. Priest. 1977. 20 Cal. 3d 25: 569 P. 2d 1303.

Index